A MANIFESTO FOR HOPE

Ten principles for transforming the lives of
children, young people and their families

Steve Chalke

First published in 2023
by SPCK

First published in Great Britain in 2023

Society for Promoting Christian Knowledge
RH101, The Record Hall, 16-16A Baldwin's Gardens,
London EC1N 7RJ
www.spck.org.uk

British Library Cataloguing-in-Publication Data
A catalogue record for this book is available from the British Library

ISBN 978-0-281-08779-2
eBook ISBN 978-0-281-8780-8

3 5 7 9 10 8 6 4

Typeset by Fakenham Prepress Solutions, Fakenham, Norfolk NR21 8NL

'This important book sets out vital steps for government, civil society and key stakeholders to create integrated care for our young people. As Steve rightly pinpoints, this strategy must be long-term, cross-party, properly funded and be drawn from the full capabilities of society. Nothing is more important for the future of our country than the present for our young people.'
Sir Tony Blair, Executive Chairman, Tony Blair Institute for Global Change, and former Prime Minister of the United Kingdom (1997–2007)

'So many people are quick to make assumptions and stereotype young people, but Steve is on a mission to change this. He is a leader in bringing politicians, policy makers, practitioners and most importantly young people themselves together to look at the reality of issues on the ground. He thrives on creating practical solutions to bring hope and change.'
Florence Eshalomi, Member of Parliament for Vauxhall, Steve's local MP

'A brilliant and practical resource, this book will help you to reimagine: communities where every child is nurtured; where families thrive; and where local charities, grassroots movements and faith groups are empowered to work in a more collaborative, less bureaucratic and far more productive relationship with both local and national government.'
Professor Kevin Fenton CBE, statutory public health advisor to the Mayor of London and the Greater London Authority and Regional Director of Public Health for NHS London

'This book will not disappoint anyone looking for new inspiration, ambition and hope that we can solve some of the most intractable social problems facing young people today. Steve draws on three decades of rich experience working in communities throughout the country – refusing to accept that change can't happen – and always holding on to the highest ambitions for our young people, whatever their background or circumstance. The stories and voices in these pages remind us how urgent the need for reform is for those young people who face high levels of disadvantage and poverty, and even the

threat of exploitation and harm. Steve challenges us all to imagine the brighter futures our young people and our communities could have and join him on a mission to change the way we deliver services to those who are often struggling the most.'
Anne Longfield CBE, former Children's Commissioner for England, and Chair of the Commission on Young Lives.

'Steve Chalke has made a lifestyle out of making good things happen in a challenging world. He has brought people together to understand what is right and just, make clear commitments to it and agree what we must do to deliver it. Our children need hope. This book helps us understand that need and how we can work together to shape policy and society to make that possible.'
Marvin Rees, Mayor of Bristol

'Steve has dedicated his life to changing young people's lives and transforming our world for the better, and he has distilled a lifetime of experience into this remarkable book. It's everything I love about Steve – bold, brave, compelling, inspirational and earthed in wisdom and experience. Steve is right: we need a revolution to build a society for all children and his manifesto for hope is a radical clarion call for change.'
Mark Russell, Chief Executive, The Children's Society

'Never have I read a book that has so much love, wisdom and common sense in every chapter! This book resonated with me in a way no book ever has before. Steve's decades of real-life experience shine through in the compassion and wisdom on every page. His manifesto for hope is just what we need right now.'
Julie Siddiqi MBE, mentor, consultant, social activist and former Executive Director of the Islamic Society of Britain.

'WOW! Everyone should read and then reread this book. It was born out of total frustration with our broken systems and a lifetime of experience, which I have watched, of swimming against the tide to create hope.'
Anthea Turner, television presenter

Contents

Dedication

To John Coldman and John Whiter without whom we could not
have come this far.

Acknowledgements

There are no words to articulate the debt I owe to all of you who
are, or who have been part of the Oasis team through the years –
staff, volunteers, students and community members – as we have
worked to bring hope to individual lives and whole communities.
I have learned so much from you all. This book, as you will recognise, is jam-packed full of your ideas.

An Introduction

It was 1 December 1942, less than a month since the Allied forces' victory in the Battle of El Alamein, a decisive turning point in the Second World War. On this day, William Beveridge, a sixty-something man who until then had been relatively unknown, published the findings of a review he had been commissioned to carry out for the British government under the rather inauspicious title of 'The Report of the Inter-Departmental Committee on Social Insurance and Allied Services'.

But this review was unusual. Ordinary people rushed in their thousands to buy a copy. In little over a year, the 'Beveridge Report' as it became known, had sold more than 600,000 copies in the UK and many more abroad, and from its 300 pages would grow one of the most talked about revolutions in history; the welfare state. In fact, publication of Beveridge's report had been delayed by several weeks because some members of the national government, led by Conservative prime minister Winston Churchill, considered it all just too revolutionary!

Driven by a quest for social justice, Beveridge believed that the UK government should do battle beyond the war against what he named as the five 'giant evils'; idleness, ignorance, disease, squalor and want. He put forward the idea that benefits should be paid to all who were sick, unemployed, retired or widowed, and allowances given to assist young families as they made their way in post-war Britain. This system, which his report called 'social security', would provide a minimum standard of living 'below which no one should be allowed to fall', and so protect the whole population from poverty. To fund this, all working people would make weekly contributions, as would employers, through the introduction of 'social insurance'. The goal of full employment would be pivotal to Beveridge's social welfare programme, for which he said the post-war state, rather than simply individual employers, should take responsibility. Lastly, and most famously, he recommended the establishment of a national health service with the aim of offering free medical treatment to all, regardless or wealth or income.

Though what he called his 'cradle to the grave' social programme alienated some, his ideas struck a real chord with the general public. And, for his critics, who worried about the cost of all this, he argued that creating the welfare institutions he recommended would increase the competitiveness of British industry, by producing healthier, wealthier and thus more motivated and productive workers who would also serve as a great source of demand for British goods. So it was that in 1945, the new post-war prime minister, Clement Attlee, announced his government would introduce the proposals set out in Beveridge's report. The welfare state was born. And, on 5 July 1948, the then Minister of Health, Aneurin Bevin, launched its crowning glory, the National Health Service.

To begin with it was all a huge success. The welfare state created new services, trained professionals, improved health and life opportunities. But only two years after the NHS was born, the first signs of stress on the system were beginning to show. In 1950, Bevan was called to parliament to explain the spiralling costs, and a year later he resigned because of the introduction of charges for dental care and spectacles. Things got worse. By the 1970s the post-war boom had disappeared. The economy was struggling and welfare bills were steadily rising. But leaders, then as now, couldn't agree on the way ahead. Many insisted that more money had to be found for success, convinced of the power of the state to serve all. Others believed that too much cash was being wasted, and that the welfare state must be slimmed down and that public–private partnerships would save the day as well as deliver more effective outcomes.

Those debates about the viability of the welfare state are now constant. Poverty and inequality have not been addressed. Instead they are growing, with the gap between the rich and poor wider than at any point since the nineteenth century. And chronic diseases, ones that Beveridge did not have in mind when he planned his revolution and that can't, or can't easily, be cured – cancers, dementia, obesity, diabetes, loneliness and mental illnesses to name a few – need the kind of funding and long-term support, which the NHS is just not set up to be able to deliver easily.

More than that, the welfare state as a whole was designed for a world where, except for temporary disruptions, jobs were expected to be for life, where most people only lived for a few years after retirement, where medicine was much more basic, and no one had ever heard of genomics or hip replacements, heart transplants or IVF, and where the concept of the 'teenager' and teenage culture had not yet been invented. It is all different now. Our post-war, twentieth-century institutions were not built for our twenty-first century world. The old orthodoxies will no longer work, and they certainly won't cope with the challenges ahead. So, instead of trying to fix them, we need a different way of thinking.

But, as we look forward, I believe that we would do well to glance back too. It was in 1946, even before the NHS was launched, that Beveridge published another report. Its theme was voluntary action. He made it clear that he believed the way in which his ideas were beginning to be implemented was bypassing the power of ordinary people in local communities; preventing them from contributing their time, energy, ideas and even their money to the services being offered. 'It did frankly send a chill to my heart', he is said to have exclaimed when he learned that all welfare services would be administered by civil servants. Beveridge was convinced that it was communities, rather than distant hierarchical authorities and institutions, that were much better at both understanding real needs and designing local workable solutions. It was essential, as he saw it, to develop strong partnership between the state and existing voluntary organisations. This level of collaboration was central to success, because neither government nor the voluntary sector alone was capable of delivering the outcomes needed. The people had to be involved.

The problem was that no one was listening. The public were already beginning to enjoy the fruit of Beveridge's first report and so had lost interest. The post-war Labour government was persuaded that the detached and depersonalised work of professionals rather than, what they believed would be, the well-meaning but emotional interventions of the unqualified, would lead to the levelling of opportunity for all.

It was a huge mistake – one that we are still paying for. It's time for another revolution. This time together. If you are interested, I invite you to read on.

Principle one
An ounce of practice is worth a ton of theory

It was New Year's Eve 2021. The emergency services – police and paramedics – had been called to a house following reports of an incident there. A little later, as evening fell, a five-year-old boy was pronounced dead. His mother, in her thirties, was detained at the scene under the Mental Health Act, and has since been charged with her son's murder, which she denies. Just under twenty-four hours earlier, another boy, a fifteen-year-old teenager, in a different town, was attacked and murdered as he walked through a park. Two boys who never knew one another, from completely different parts of the country, lost their lives in completely different circumstances. Two lives brimming with potential, ended needlessly.

Out of those two tragic events – those twenty-four hours – the idea for this book was born.

Perhaps all that these boys had in common is that they were both students at schools run by Oasis, the charity I began and still work for. 'Oasis exists to build healthy communities where everyone can thrive and achieve their God-given potential', says our founding document. But for these two boys we failed to be able to fulfil our promise.

In both communities, time after time, Oasis had applied with no success for the resources to develop a more joined-up model of children's, youth and family work: a model which has brought extraordinary results in other areas of the country where we have been able to fund it.

Were there chances missed to intervene to potentially save these young lives? Was it a lack of funding that cost them their futures? If more money had been available would things have been different? Or is there more to it than just that? Could Oasis have done more? What more might social services, mental health services, the police, local authorities, central government or community leaders have done? Not just for these two boys, but for the long-term life opportunities and welfare of many more.

How do we close the gaps in 'the system'? Is there more that we can do to stop children, teenagers and sometimes whole families 'slipping through the net'? How can we reduce the cost borne, not just by the families involved directly, but by whole communities and wider society, both socially and economically? It is said that change is the end result of all true learning. If that is true, what do we know and what can we learn?

That is what this book is about.

- We know our first task as a society is to care for our children – a task so fundamental that if we do not get it right, then we will struggle to get anything else right.
- We know that real safety for any one of our children is dependent on creating a society where every child is cared for, nurtured and safe.
- We know that, although childhood should be a safe harbour, wide and persistent gaps in children's development open up along socio-economic lines from an early age.
- We know that if you grow up in poverty, you'll have fewer opportunities to live a healthy, prosperous life. And that babies from poorer households are more likely to have a lower birth weight, a less stimulating home learning environment, and are more likely to develop social, emotional and behavioural

problems. We know that behavioural problems in childhood are predictive of later and continued involvement in crime and antisocial behaviour.

- We know that there are communities across our country where we are completely failing to protect vulnerable children from the ongoing epidemic of county lines, criminal exploitation and serious violence.
- We know that, though those from wealthy homes in leafy suburbs are not immune, this failure disproportionately impacts poorer households, and those from black as well as various other majority ethnic young people.
- We know that if young people socialise in safe and protective schools and community settings, they will be supported to form safe and protective peer relationships. But if they form friendships in contexts characterised by violence and harmful attitudes, these relationships are likely to be unsafe and promote antisocial behaviour as a means of navigating, or surviving in, those relationships.

But we also know that for far too many families and communities our current system just isn't working. To seek to turn our backs on this reality has to be the equivalent to being a climate-change denier. Our hospitals are overwhelmed. Our GPs are overstretched. Our social services can't cope. Our education system is creaking at the seams. Many suggest that this is simply the result of long-term underfunding. I disagree. No one would suggest that more investment isn't needed. But the issue is deeper than that. Even more than the money, we need a bold and radical new approach. Business as usual will not do. We may need more money, but we definitely need better-spent money. Better priorities would save a fortune. We need a completely new way of working: we need a revolution. Investment, on its own, is a short-term fix, and short-term fixes very often stop us searching hard enough for long-term solutions.

On the one hand, successive governments over decades have built a wide range of binding operational rules and regulations governing the various statutory services that just don't fit with one another. On the other, local charities which are doing great work are badly funded, forced to compete for short-term grants and contracts and are measured by equally short-term and superficial outcomes rather than any real, substantial and sustainable long-term benefit. Added to this, whether we choose to acknowledge it or not, various groups of children within our society far too often find themselves marginalised and discriminated against. From sections of our Black and Asian communities, travellers, looked-after children, those who are neuro-divergent, and those with learning difficulties, to those who are physically disabled, or LGBT+, or Muslim…the list is a long one.

Everything is interconnected.

Later this year, Oasis will open Oasis Restore, England's first secure school; an innovative, new model of care for children aged twelve to eighteen who have been sentenced to custody by the courts or are being held on remand.[1] With education and healthcare at its heart, as young people placed at Oasis Restore are enabled to come to terms with the consequences of their criminal behaviour, our job is also to slowly come to understand the stories behind those actions, and to help them build the skills they need to lead positive and productive future lives.

We are excited, but here is the issue – the justice system sits at the end of a long line of other systems: education, housing and town planning, social services, health and mental-health care and so on. So, for example, as long as education continues to be the narrow, ill-fitting straitjacket that fails to recognise the skills and needs of children who are atypical, too many of them will keep falling out of mainstream education, into the arms of serious organised crime; eventually ending up in the morgue or the justice system, whatever

---

1 Oasis was appointed in 2018 to open and deliver the first secure school, by the Ministry of Justice.

we at Oasis Restore or others in any other custodial setting do. This book hopes to make a difference. But, who is it for?

It's for government – both central and local. It's for politicians of all colours, shades and hues. It's for policy makers and practitioners. It's for business leaders. It's for statutory agencies and charities, for grassroots organisations and faith groups, for passionate individuals and all who long for things to be different. Or, to put it into the words of the ancient Hebrew prophet in Isaiah, which became the celebrated theme of Dr Martin Luther King Jr, it's for all those who long for the day when, 'Every valley shall be raised up, every mountain and hill made low; the rough ground shall become level, the rugged places a plain.'[2]

There are countless commentaries and research papers, some very good, some superficial, on the reasons for the failure of the system. The primary aim of this book is not to add to them. Rather, its goal is to prompt discussion and action about a new vision to offer a more hopeful solution.

The famous Greek poet Hesiod, who lived back in the eighth century BC, wrote an epic poem called *Works and Days,* which contains the story of Pandora's box. Zeus, the king of all the gods, is angry because Prometheus, the god of fire, has stolen fire from heaven and given it to humanity. Zeus believes that Prometheus's 'gift' has given humans too much power. So, he decides to seek revenge and put humanity back in its place. And, with help from some of his colleagues, he creates Pandora.

Pandora is intensely beautiful, but deceptive and with a heart of stone, and Zeus has a mission for her. He sends her to the Greek king with a box: Pandora's box. He orders her to open the box, out of which fly all sorts of evils: drought, famine, plague, pestilence, death and suffering. Then he orders the box to be shut, just before

---

2 Isaiah 40:4, NIV.

the last 'gift' can escape it. That last gift is hope. Hope is trapped deliberately in the box. People can deal with pestilence, plague and pandemics, but without hope, they are lost. From then on, over the centuries that followed, it was left to Greek thinkers and philosophers to debate what they believed it meant for hope to be locked away from humanity. The great thinker Plato explained that, as far as he could see, hope is real, but it is distant. In this world, hope stays in the box, he asserts. Only as we finally 'escape' this life can we encounter the reality of hope. It is, as some would say, 'pie in the sky when you die'. For others, it seemed it was a very good job that hope was locked in the box: the availability of hope only makes people lazy; success in life is about pulling yourself up by your own bootstraps; we are all self-determining; we have a responsibility to take control; hard work liberates; hope simply creates lethargy...

I believe that the choices we make and decisions we take can release hope from its box: for ourselves, for others, for our communities and for society at large. The question is what will it take to prise the lid off? Years ago, an astute old friend of mine explained a principle that I have benefited from every single day since I first heard it. 'In theory,' she said, 'practice is the same as theory, but in practice, theory and practice are rarely related.'

When I left school, I wanted to go to college. But a wise friend advised me that before I even thought of that, I should move to what was then a pretty tough and run-down housing estate, set up and lead a youth club, and pay for it all by getting a manual job in a local factory as a cleaner for a couple of years. I took his advice. Fifty years later, I am still glad I did it. It was the foundation of everything I've been able to build since then.

Put differently, in order to understand anything about community development in general, you must first have experienced it, long-term, in micro-detail, in at least one real local community. You are guaranteed to have a much more profound contribution to bring to the boardroom or the cabinet meeting room as a result of having first sat in lots of diverse front rooms, right in the heart of family homes.

Take an example from the world of education.

Recently, a government minister – no doubt inspired by a group of special advisors – suggested that parents who fail to ensure that their children attend school regularly could have their child benefit payments stopped. He argued that because it is often the case that absenteeism leads to involvement in antisocial behaviour, we need to get back to an 'absolute rigorous focus on school attendance', and that such penalties would help restore what he called 'an ethic of responsibility'.

There is a famous line in *Harry Potter and the Order of the Phoenix*, the fifth book in the extremely popular series of novels by J. K. Rowling. Dolores Umbridge, a British Ministry of Magic bureaucrat, is installed as a 'defence against the dark arts' teacher at Hogwarts School of Wizardry. In the very first lesson she takes for Harry's class she explains to her students, 'It is the view of the Ministry that a theoretical knowledge will be sufficient'. The point is, of course, it wasn't. A theoretical knowledge alone never is.

It reminded me of the story of Sammy, a thirteen-year-old who would often fail to attend school and even when she did arrive would normally be late, turn up not wearing the correct uniform, and then prove to be distracted and inattentive in class.

Sammy was constantly given detentions, which made her angry and uncooperative, and led to more detentions and very poor rela-tionships with the school staff. Then a new and highly experienced headteacher arrived at the school, and being told of Sammy's track-record, he made a decision.

The new head invited Sammy to spend a breaktime with him. As the two of them talked, he discovered that almost two years before, Sammy's mother – a single parent following the death of her husband – had suffered a breakdown in her mental health, but was unable to get the professional support that she needed to cope. Instead, Sammy's grandmother shouldered the responsibility of helping Sammy's mother with Sammy and two younger siblings.

But now, the grandmother was long-term ill herself, and unable to give any help in the mornings. So instead each school day, Sammy would get her two younger siblings up, get them showered and dressed, make them breakfast, prepare them a packed lunch and walk them to their primary school, all before coming to school herself. However, sometimes she was so worried about her mum, she would feel that she had to go home instead to get her up and look after her.

The detentions were stopped. Sammy was given personalised support with her learning. The school intervened and talked with the local social services and adult mental health team to ensure that Sammy's mum began to receive the care she needed. That summer Sammy was awarded the school prize for resilience. She is now at university, and her mum is doing much better and is back in full-time employment.

Over the years I've listened to many academics who preach on the importance of study and theory, which can then be applied to subsequent practice. The problem is that all that produces is what is known as shallow learning. What is known as deep learning grows out of experience or, put differently, practice on which we then reflect and build relevant theory. That experienced-based theory is subsequently put into practice, and the cycle begins again; the more experience, the more reflection, the deeper the learning.

Shallow learning centres around the amassing and retention of theoretical information, but this becomes an undigested burden until it is understood. And in a worst-case scenario can result in an 'I'm-only-obeying-orders' syndrome. Conversely, deep learning is about wisdom gained from wide-awake, first-hand, real-time experience; wisdom which slowly becomes fundamental to the identity of the person of the learner. Deep learning is the wisdom of the child learning to talk, the jazz pianist, the gold medal athlete and the expert kitchen fitter. It's the characteristic of the Formula One motor racing driver, the sculptor and the Macmillan nurse, the community development worker, or the footballer who, just like David Beckham once did, can 'bend' a football in a dramatic, sometimes uncanny, curve through the air from a free kick. Where shallow learning is playing the right notes; deep learning enables a beautiful performance. And where shallow learning gives access to vocabulary and the rules of grammar; deep learning creates masterful poetry. Deep learning moves us from the superficial 'knowledge' and introduces us to authentic personal wisdom. It brings to those who develop it a vitality, a dynamism, and a depth and breadth of multifaceted understanding that desk-top, academic learning lacks.

I doubt that David Beckham gives many lectures on physics, his understanding of the various aerodynamic forces around a spinning ball, the Magnus effect, and air pressure variants on a football in flight or wake deflection. But I bet he has a lot to say about the long hours of training on a football pitch that allowed him to learn to bend the ball and steal the match.

You can't learn to ride a bike by studying geometry, but only by getting on one and peddling. Deep learning is about that – and sometimes about falling off.

It's not that the theory is unimportant, but that it is vital it follows and serves the practice rather than dictates to and dominates it. In fact, renowned psychologist and educationalist David Kolb is famous because of the four-stage learning cycle through which he observed the most meaningful and effective learning happens:

Stage 1: Having a concrete, real-time experience
Stage 2: Reflecting on that experience

Stage 3: Concluding from the experience
Stage 4: Acting differently as a result of the experience.[3]

I set up what is now known as the Oasis Charitable Trust back in September 1985. I had left my job the previous month with a vision to build strong and vibrant local communities; specifically to develop supported housing for young people, as well as primary and secondary schools that nurtured children, and to create accessible healthcare. I was twenty-nine and had no funding, no salary, no savings (though my wife and I were given free housing for twelve months) and no contacts.

It was a tough year, but we survived it and through it Oasis was born. Now, almost forty years later, Oasis has grown to become one of the biggest charities in the UK. We work in local communities across England as well as in other countries around the world. Here in the UK we employ around 6,000 people as well as thousands of volunteers. We provide housing, education, healthcare; we work in youth justice, as well as run churches and many other local community-building initiatives. We work in partnership (and sometimes tension!) with central and local government, as well as with hundreds of other charities and businesses large and small, but most importantly with countless local, community-led, grassroots initiatives, churches and other faith groups, and individuals. And through it all, via endless mistakes and sometimes life-and-death struggles, we have slowly learned what I believe are the keys to effective and sustainable community development. So, this book sets out our ten core principles.

- Ten principles that focus on the needs of the whole person, in the context of their whole life and the whole community.
- Ten principles at the core of all successful and sustainable community development work.

---

3 David Allen Kolb, an American educationalist, published his seminal experiential learning theory (ELT) in 1984, which set out the four-stage learning cycle.

- Ten principles that demonstrate 'why' it is essential we rethink our entire social and welfare system to engage and empower those local communities, rather than doing the same thing over and over and expecting a different result. Principles that are designed to shift the relentless focus on the measurement of short-term, expensive and siloed 'interventions' (I hate that term), towards longer-term 'engagement' and 'partnership' and investment in more meaningful, locally owned community development.
- Ten principles for joined-up government and joined-up services for joined-up people.
- Ten principles that I've tried to make as sequential as possible, though, as you'll discover, they are interwoven and interconnected and I have interspersed them with the stories of children, young people and their families with whom we have come into contact. Stories of success; stories of frustration; stories to learn from.
- Ten principles that sit at the heart of Oasis' mission and have been gleaned from almost four decades of hard-won experience. Principles that are accompanied by a ten-point manifesto, because as the terrifying universal law of entropy states: left unchecked, disorder increases, energy disperses and systems dissolve into chaos.

And the fact that an ounce of practice is worth a ton of theory is the first of them!

So, all that having been said, in the words of my friend and veteran US social activist, Jim Wallis: 'You change society by changing the wind. Change the wind, transform the debate, recast the discussion, alter the context in which political discussions are being made, and you will change the outcomes.' That's the aim of this book – it's a heartfelt call for the creation of a system that works for all children, young people and their families – it's a manifesto for hope!

Principle two
Where there's ruin, there's hope

'We are all in the same storm, but in very different boats.' That was the cry throughout the two years of Covid. And it's just as true, if not more so, now. Just like its predecessor, the new pandemic – the cost-of-living crisis – is amplifying the fault lines that already existed in our society, creating in its wake a left-out generation who, if we do not act now, will never recover from the wounds it inflicts on them. While some have yachts, some are forced to get by with canoes or on life-rafts supplied by others. And countless thousands of the most vulnerable families and their children across the UK are drowning.

'Never let a serious crisis go to waste. It's an opportunity to do things you thought you could not do before,' became a popular way of thinking during the pandemic. As the memory of Covid 19 slowly recedes into the distance, we must learn from the experience of having lived through it: lessons that, if learned, will help us steer through the storms that inevitably still lie ahead of us. Put differently, what are the principles that we can salvage from the turbulence of recent years that will better equip our society to sail more confidently and successfully beyond our current horizon?

As I sat down to begin to write this book, a community worker friend of mine told me a story about the summer holiday hunger club they'd just finished running. She explained that after eating a hot dog he was given, one little boy quietly came up to her and asked if he could take something for his brother who was at home and was hungry too.

It's often claimed, in the phrase I quoted in the first chapter, that 'the system is broken' – that the current model of welfare, care and protection is failing countless thousands of the most vulnerable children and their families across the UK that it was designed to serve.

I believe that this is the wrong diagnosis. It hides the truth. The situation is far worse than that.

It is not that the system is broken and isn't working; it is that there is no system. There never was a system. What we actually have is a collection of different systems – social care, education, family support, health, mental health, housing, justice – that are not joined up. Instead, they all operate independently. They function within different frameworks, they are top down and bureaucratic, they are overly fixated on process, they collect different data, they're 'output' obsessed (How many clients have we been involved with/calls have we answered?) rather than 'outcome' focused (What difference did we make?) and there's no effective interface between them, so any unifying sense of shared and focused vision and purpose is non-existent. The irony in all this is that, in a sense, many of these systems – in their own terms – aren't broken at all. The terrible truth is that although they are dysfunctional, they are all doing exactly what they have been designed to do. That is the elephant in the room!

I want to be very clear that there is no question that each of these systems is filled with countless hardworking, kind, capable and creative, overstretched and underfunded people. These wonderful people, whom we clapped and banged saucepans for every Thursday evening at 7 p.m. back in 2020, are not the problem – they are an extraordinary asset. The issue lies elsewhere.

It's not just that the individual systems lack cohesion; many are not even connected and joined up within themselves. Instead, they're made up of various smaller, disjointed systems, each run by its own set of managers. Over the last twenty years, part of my job has been to engage with both central and local government departments – a task in which I never cease to be amazed by the level of muddle and confusion, poor communication, institutional deafness to the complexity of need, and the huge levels of unnecessary expenditure. One senior civil servant memorably explained to me that their department is like 'a car with the engine of a lawn mower, the brakes of a Formula One racing car, and no driver'. In my experience, if a local charity or business operated in this way, it would be bust within months.

A few weeks ago, a secondary school headteacher wrote to me:

> *On Monday I took a Year 7 boy home who was unwell. He had not eaten for two days and when I went into the family home, there were seven of them living in a two-bedroomed house, all of them unwell and hungry. I bought food and sanitary products for the family for a week and showed the mum what meals she could make from the ingredients. The reality is that this was just one family I was able to help for a short amount of time, but we have many, many families in this situation.*

> *The health of people in this community is so poor; the level of deprivation is high and the rate of crime, abuse, domestic violence and neglect is sometimes too hard to comprehend.*

The tragedy is that it is because the individual statutory systems, with their various rules and regulations, don't fit together they create the very gaps that fail the families they are trying to support. And none of this is helped by the constantly shifting policies and changing targets that go with them, overlaid with the endless churn of staff changing roles and the acute lack of organisational memory that accompanies all this.

It's a bit like the pieces of a jigsaw puzzle that you struggle for hours to put together, before eventually realising that it's impossible. Not only do they not fit; they will never fit because they don't belong to the same picture. So, even if you do manage to push them together in a makeshift and awkward way, there will always be gaps between them.

That's why we have to think differently. It is impossible to solve our current problems with the same thinking that created them. More money might be needed, but the crisis we face is not primarily about underinvestment. Better management may be needed, but the issues we must confront are not primarily about poor management. Instead, we need a root-and-branch revolution. Everything has to change.

We need a radical reset – an urgent overhaul – of all the systems and the way that they interact. We have to address some fundamental principles. Some holy shibboleths, though taken for granted, have to be challenged. Only this will transform the life chances of thousands of vulnerable young people and their families, whereas our failure to do so will come at huge cost to us all, both socially and economically, in the years to come.

In my view, our problem is that we have the wrong kind of thinking. We need a new vision of the way society works. Bluntly put, though we need great 'system leaders', we have an even greater need for visionary 'cross-system leaders'. Leaders who, though they may not be egoless, can understand and control their own ego-driven habits, allowing them to think, work and plan together.

We need one well-organised, integrated and holistic system of care for children and their families that is truly aligned and attuned to the real needs of those it seeks to serve.

Slow evolution will not do. We need a new model now; a care system that cares. One that is fit for purpose and – notwithstanding more investment – not as wasteful of the precious resources, both human and financial, which are already available. Indeed, unless we achieve that, however much cash we throw at what we have now, little will change.

We can do this, but we have to do it together.

At Oasis, we know we have a long way to go, but although the complexity of our operation now means that we are legally compelled to operate as a number of national charities – each with its own board, chief executive, senior staff team and formal responsibilities – we have worked very hard to ensure that we have also maintained one shared vision, one shared framework, one joint strategy, one common purpose, one shared accountability, and the mechanisms to make this work.

When leaders of different agencies are willing to be held accountable to a single framework of common purpose, all of the services they offer will be more targeted and more efficient. The sum will be greater than the parts. Staff delivering the various services will work together rather than in silos or in competition; communication with those they seek to serve will be more coordinated; decisions about services will not be at odds with one another; budgets will not be duplicated, and therefore the money available to support communities will be maximised instead of wasted.

Ironically, the mix of ill-fitting statutory systems we have at the moment disempowers the staff working within them as much as it does the individuals and families it seeks to serve – creating a toxicity which is traumatising for all who are touched by it. While the office manuals of the various statutory services stifle the transformational work for which they exist, those they work with feel like 'cases' to be dealt with rather than people to be understood. Hence, the huge number of vacancies in so many of the vocational services, such as the National Health Service or teaching. Staff find themselves broken by a bureaucracy that saps them of energy and leaves them disillusioned.

Under the present model, the vast majority of individuals and families at risk who come into contact with the statutory services never move on from dependency. At the same time, many far more poorly funded voluntary sector agencies deliver more 'bang for each buck' and are far more successful in terms of the long-term empowerment they deliver.

I remember talking to a senior employee of a city council, who had previously worked within a third-sector development agency, and was simply stunned by the reduced expectation of change or progress in his new working environment.

As I have said, it took two tragic deaths – one of an innocent teenager in a park, the other of a blameless child – to precipitate the writing of this book. But as I write, millions of children across the UK are being condemned to a lifetime of struggle, to which Britain has no meaningful response. The chronic failure to safeguard vulnerable children continues as police and social care teams simply don't have the resources to keep up. Those who are being abused know they are being harmed often long before someone else notices their needs, but there is no one to help. Children trapped in abusive relationships or groomed into criminal gangs harm themselves and others. Parents find themselves in situations where they can't cope and yet feel alone and with no way of finding or accessing the support they need. Others are anxious about the safety of their children, but don't know what to do or where to turn.

At the start of the Covid pandemic in 2020, it was estimated that 40% of children were part of a family that was unable to afford a decent standard of living and were being forced to forgo material necessities. For the poorest 10% of families, food and fuel were already taking up the vast majority of their income after housing costs. If life were a game of football, these children and their families were already 10-nil down, even before the recession struck. But since then the situation has deteriorated much further. As prices have soared and cuts have been made, millions more have fallen into poverty. Children go to school ill-clad and undernourished. Stress and anxiety eat away at the resilience of families. Parents choose whether to feed their electricity meters or themselves.

The cruelty of life dictates that while some are cushioned, those hardest hit by the cost-of-living crisis are those who had less money in the first place. More than that, because of the huge amounts of time and energy they have to devote to survival, the poorest are also the ones who have least time to devote to thinking about their future and planning for it.

Those of us with eyes to see – from those in national or local government, those in national charities or statutory services, through to the pavement-level voluntary sector and individual community members – find ourselves sitting on a social, emotional, mental-health and economic time-bomb. If we are going to improve children's life chances or deliver assistance, it's time to reimagine. We need a mind-set change which will cascade into a better, more joined-up, integrated, holistic and robust approach to building safe communities for children and their families, where all feel safe, have ownership and can thrive.

A great example of this can be seen in a story told to me by an architect friend of mine. He swears it is true, but I like to think of it as the parable of the swimming pool!

The local town council had a problem. The population of the housing estate on the edge of town had very poor health outcomes, and the records showed that right across the age range the residents made little use of the gym and swimming pool facility about a mile down the main road. The leisure centre had a very dated feel and the town leaders felt that this was the problem. So they hired a team of architects. What could be done to improve the situation? Would it be possible to redesign the facade? Remodel the pool? Re-equip the gym to attract more footfall? Perhaps the whole building would need to be rebuilt?

After some months of work, the architects reported back. The council chamber was full, and with a real sense of anticipation the councillors awaited the ideas and designs. The senior architect addressed them. 'Ladies and gentlemen,' she began. 'You commissioned our team to work on ideas which would make your leisure centre more attractive to the population of the housing estate, who rarely use it and struggle with health problems. We have researched a number of ideas – from recladding the building to demolishing and rebuilding it completely – and consulted extensively with the community involved. So, we are pleased to present our recommended approach to this issue.'

Then she unveiled a picture. But instead of the spectacular design that the councillors were expecting to see, it was... a giant print of the bus timetable. 'While we are obviously happy for you to pay us however much you would like to rebuild your sports facility,' the architect responded to her audience's obvious disappointment, 'a much cheaper approach would be to rethink and improve the bus timetable, so that the residents of the estate are able to get to and from the centre at times that work with their lifestyles and responsibilities.'

This was a classic case of asking the wrong set of questions, based on the wrong assumptions, which framed the wrong debate and almost resulted in a very expensive solution that would have been destined to fail. What is known in some circles as an epistemological error![4]

Anne Longfield, the former Children's Commissioner for England, has talked about the cliff edge facing many of the most vulnerable children in our society, while Amanda Spielman, the Chief Inspector of Ofsted through the Covid pandemic, warned us that we are looking at a whole generation of lost young people.

---

4 Epistemology is the study of the mind's relation to reality. Its job is to seek to answer questions such as, 'What is knowledge?' and 'How is our knowledge acquired?', or in plain language 'How do we avoid framing the problems wrongly?'

How do we stop children falling over that cliff edge? How do government, local authorities, statutory services, big charities, local community and faith groups, grassroots alliances and individual local people who care, all work together to prevent this disaster?

We know the immediate and short-term consequences of rising poverty: more malnourishment, children going to school on empty stomachs; more unemployment; more depression; more poor mental health; more physical health implications; more domestic tension and violence; more family breakups; more homelessness and more children in care. But long term, the psychological scars of poverty run even deeper, as the inequalities compound. They are confidence-destroying. They are socially inhibiting. The wounds caused by exclusion are there for ever: a feeling that you can never identify with your peer group or neighbours on equal terms, a reticence about involving yourself in larger groups or community activities and a suspicion of situations that leave you insecure.

Coronavirus and the present cost-of-living crisis aside, however, none of this is new. 'Fair Society, Healthy Lives', better known as the Marmot Review, was published back in 2010.[5] In it, Professor Sir Michael Marmot explored the reasons for the health inequalities which plagued England at the time, though the same could have been said for the whole of the UK. It was a landmark piece of work. Particularly focused on the field of healthcare, it proposed a strategy to address and reduce inequalities in what it called the 'social determinants of health': the conditions in which people are born, grow, live, work and age. It made a robust, passionate and very well-evidenced business case for both national and local action to address these inequalities through a concerted, determined strategy to create a fair society and a healthier life for all.

---

5 In November 2008, Professor Sir Michael Marmot was asked by the then Secretary of State for Health to chair an independent review to propose the most effective evidence-based strategies for reducing health inequalities in England from 2010. The final report, 'Fair Society, Healthy Lives', was published on 11 February 2010. You can find the full report on the Marmot Review website at: https://www.instituteofhealthequity.org/resources-reports/fair-society-healthy-lives-the-marmot-review.

It found that most people in England weren't living as long as the best off, and that premature illness and death affected everyone below those at the top of society. Even more disturbingly, it showed that disadvantage started before birth and accumulated throughout life, and that the lower a person's social and economic status, the poorer their health was likely to be.

Shockingly, people living in the poorest communities in the country died, on average, seven years earlier than those in the richest neighbourhoods, but also spent longer in those shorter lives battling with ill-health and disability: on average a staggering seventeen years less of health and life. However, it also made it clear that it wasn't just the situation of the bottom 10% that should be focused on, because there are poorer outcomes all the way down from the top.

It also demonstrated that, traditionally, government policies have focused resources only on some segments of society, whereas to reduce unfair and unjust inequalities in health, action was needed across what it called the whole social gradient. However, the level of action should be matched with a scale and intensity that was proportionate to the level of disadvantage.

It said that these health inequalities arose from a complex inter-action of many factors – housing, employment, educational attainment, quality of neighbourhood, social isolation, disability – all of which are strongly affected by one's economic and social status. It spelt out that action was needed across all these areas. It suggested that health inequalities were largely preventable, arguing that not only was there a strong social justice case for addressing health inequalities, but also a pressing economic one. It estimated that the annual cost of health inequalities, even at that time, stood at around £40 billion through lost taxes, welfare payments and costs to the NHS. But here is the key point: Marmot argued that 'the' key to addressing health inequalities was the creation of the conditions for people to take control of their own lives, and that the voluntary and private sectors had a vital and pivotal role to play in this as partners alongside government and the statutory sector.

It set out a framework for action with two big societal goals:

1 To create an enabling society that maximises individual and community potential.
2 To ensure social justice, health and sustainability sit at the heart of all government policies.

Finally, to achieve these goals, it set out six policy objectives, with the highest priority being given to the first:

• Giving every child the best start in life.
• Enabling all children, young people and adults to maximise their capabilities and have control over their lives.
• Creating and developing sustainable places and communities.
• Strengthening the role and impact of ill-health prevention.
• Creating fair employment and good work for all.
• Ensuring a healthy standard of living for all.

But here is the tragedy. Ten years later, Sir Michael's follow-up report, published in 2020, found that rather than making any progress, for the first time in more than 100 years, life expectancy had failed to increase across the country. More than that, health inequalities had widened overall; the social gradient had become even steeper, children's and youth centres had closed, funding for education had been reduced, a housing crisis and a rise in homelessness had developed, a growing number of households had insufficient money to lead a healthy life, and a greater number of local communities had slipped into despair. The overall result: child poverty had significantly increased rather than decreased. And, underpinning all this, came the same message as a decade before: central to addressing each of these health inequalities remains the creation of an environment where people can take control of their own lives.

This is the role of local communities – of local grassroots movements, faith groups and individuals – supported, resourced and partnering with big charities and big business, government and the statutory sector.

The voice of the greatest social asset: local people – mums, dads, families, and other community members – is too often ignored. The very people the 'systems' are set up to help are unheard and alienated from them. That's why we need a radical reset.

We need a new social covenant that empowers ordinary people. The politicians tell us that the last thing they want is a 'nanny state', but a nanny state is exactly what we have. It's high time for a more mature partnership between government, local authorities and local neighbourhoods.

The voluntary sector is the hidden gem at the heart of all this: the grassroots groups, faith communities, ordinary people. It's time that the people really were allowed to 'take back control'. Only this will transform the life chances of countless young people, families and local communities. Nothing else will work, however many noughts there are at the end of the budget.

It was Rumi, the great thirteenth-century Persian poet, scholar and theologian, who first claimed, 'Where there is ruin, there is also hope'. As all these reports from the last decade and a half tell us – we know the problem we face. We don't need any more analysis. Instead, what we need is the courage to take action and create hope.

Principle three

You go faster alone, but you can go further together

It was on Monday 19 July 2010, just six months after Michael Marmot's review and perhaps in an attempt to respond to it, that 'The Big Society Network' was launched, with a fanfare of a speech by David Cameron at Liverpool Hope University. This was the new UK Prime Minister's flagship initiative, which he described as 'a national campaign for social change… run by the people, for the people'.

> *We want to give citizens, communities and local government the power and information they need to come together, solve the problems they face and build the Britain they want. We want society – the families, networks, neighbourhoods and communities that form the fabric of so much of our everyday lives – to be bigger and stronger than ever before. Only when people and communities are given more power and take more responsibility can we achieve fairness and opportunity for all.*[6]

There are 93,000 square miles in the UK, according to the Big Society website. 'The Big Society Network is about enabling you to make changes in the square mile where you live and/or work.'

It was a great ambition. They were on to something.

---

6 View at: https://assets.publishing.service.gov.uk/government/uploads/system/uploads/attachment_data/file/78979/building-big-society_0.pdf.

But, four years later, The Big Society Network collapsed. And on 24 April 2015, its founding CEO, Paul Twivy, who had resigned after just one year in post, was interviewed on the BBC Radio 4 *Today* programme. He was asked by presenter James Naughtie why it didn't work.[7]

Many had argued it was simply too vague and lacked focus. But, having lived through it as a charity leader struggling to create local empowerment, perhaps the problem was that in the end it turned out to be more of a 'big imposition' than anything else. As I talked with people – young and old – in the communities in which Oasis is based, I heard the same cries time after time. 'Give us a voice!' 'Listen to us.' 'Give us agency.' 'We feel disempowered.' 'We feel unheard.' 'Work with us.' 'Involve us.' 'Give us choice.'

Paul Twivy's own answer to James Naughtie's question was in line with just that. 'It was a series of broken promises,' he said, explaining that in his view the UK had one of the most centralised governments in the developed world and that needed to change. He concluded that we need a government 'that is going to appeal to us as human beings, not just as units of GDP. Those things aren't happening so we need to reform.'[8]

Successful 'big societies' are, of course, made up of lots of 'small communities'. According to Michael Marmot, this is all about the creation of an environment where people are allowed to take responsibility for their own lives, with local grassroots movements, individuals and big charities, alongside large companies and small businesses all being given key roles as real partners by government and the statutory sector. We desperately need that system reset. And one of the issues at the heart of it all, as Josh McCallister's 2022 independent review of the children's social care system put it, is

---

7 24 April 2015.

8 https://www.pioneerspost.com/news-views/20150424/big-society-networks-failure-down-broken-promises

that we have fallen into the trap of trying to 'replace organic bonds and relationships with professionals and services'.

The morning after the National Health Service celebrated its 70th birthday, back in July 2018, I was asked to give a keynote address to a gathered group of health leaders in London, entitled 'The Next 70 Years'. I congratulated them that in just seven short decades they had revolutionised healthcare; from hip replacements and heart transplants to IVF and gene therapy. But, I added, the reality is that this ground-breaking, world-class organisation has become a victim of its own extraordinary success. Every new medical breakthrough means more of us live longer and we create an ever-increasing strain on finite resources. So, how do we equip the NHS for the next seventy years of its journey?

I made the point that all the research shows that the vast majority of the factors that define our health are down, not so much to the work of the NHS, but to everyone else; from local councils to charities, schools to faith groups, businesses to families and individual residents.

Just days earlier, new research figures had been released around the wider determinants of health by Public Health England. And they were thought-provoking. They claimed that 'clinical care' – that's our access to a GP and a hospital, and the quality of that provision – accounts for just 20% of our health. But that our 'socio-economic' situation – our education, employment, income, family support and community safety – contributes a massive 40% of our overall score, while our 'health behaviours' – smoking, diet, exercise, alcohol consumption and sexual health – account for another 30%. Finally, our 'built environment' – the design and quality of our housing and wider physical environment – contributes the last 10%.

I explained that it could be argued, therefore, that what we call the National Health Service would be better labelled the 'National

Sickness Service'. The point at which any one of us engages with it is when we are ill. When do you make an appointment with the GP? When do you go to the hospital or see a specialist? When you are sick or have a health emergency! What we most need, therefore, is a second service to help people stay healthy and to fulfil a complementary role alongside the existing NHS. And that service must be holistic.

I chat regularly with GPs who lament that more than half of the patients they see don't come to them with any biomedical problem at all. Instead, their issues are to do with housing, children, education, employment, debt, relationships, lack of self-worth, despair and loneliness. Our problem is that we have over medicalised healthcare, focusing our thinking, energy and funding far too narrowly. It's time to think differently and invest in the other pillars on which real health and wellbeing are built. Health is three dimensional: it is about body, mind and spirit. That's why the NHS alone cannot solve the health problems of the UK. It is time to think more radically.

For the last ten years, Oasis has run a small community farm in Waterloo on an acre or so of land, which is owned and kindly leased to us by the local hospital at a peppercorn rent. Until we set up our partnership, this patch of land was a stinking, overgrown, rat-infested dumping ground; an eyesore for local residents and an embarrassment for the hospital. But, on a peppercorn rent and working with an army of volunteers, we transformed this unsightly carbuncle into a flourishing city farm, complete with goats, sheep, pigs and chickens, vegetable beds, a country garden, a camp firepit area, an outdoor kitchen, and a wonderful barn to host community events.

And still today, the farm's success remains reliant on that intrepid team of volunteers who roll up their sleeves to look after the land and care for the animals. But it's a two-way street. For instance, one of our most faithful volunteers was almost housebound before the farm opened; lonely, depressed and constantly on various prescribed drugs from her GP. 'Oasis Farm transformed my life,' she says. 'And it's saved the NHS a fortune in tablets and time!'

She is just one of a host of volunteers whose quality of life has been enhanced physically, mentally and socially by that farm. The NHS has saved valuable public funding, not just in medical bills, but also in not having to answer endless complaints about the land from local residents, who now, instead of looking out on a rubbish dump, wake up to the beauty of their new farm view, the occasional bleating of a sheep and the cock-a-doodle-dooing of a rooster. All much more therapeutic!

More than that, the whole community has gained an asset where people meet, form friendships and a new sense of purpose. The local schools also integrate the farm into their curriculums, and it can become a place of peace and sanctuary for children and young people who sometimes struggle with the environment of a full classroom and need a little space and individualised attention to re-establish their sense of calm. We call it farming therapy.

It's a real win–win–win–win situation: for the hospital, the local community, Oasis and the NHS! Communities work, and are far safer, when everyone within them is given the opportunity of getting involved and working together.

The birth of the NHS in 1948, under the visionary leadership of Nye Bevan, was revolutionary with its free and accessible health-care for all. Before then, healthcare across the country was patchy; a postcode lottery before postcodes ever existed. Churches and other voluntary groups did the best they could, while for the wealthy there were always other options. However, there was no blanket coverage or consistent quality. Then, with the formation of the NHS, the responsibility was suddenly in the hands of the government.

I remember a conversation in Downing Street with Tony Blair, then the Prime Minister, almost twenty years ago about all of this. The conversation about the stress on the NHS is not a new one!

Using the metaphor of being responsible for holding the baby, he explained to me the pressure that this sudden change of roles had created for government. I explained to him that the impact of replacing the work of voluntary bodies with that of a vast team of government-paid workers also had another unforeseen outcome – it had left the churches and other charities feeling sidelined and redundant; it robbed them of their *raison d'être*.

The tell-tale signs of the stress of this new settlement were soon all too evident. Demand instantly outstripped anything that had been forecast or planned for and costs escalated, doubling and trebling in the first few years. And when Hugh Gaitskell, then Chancellor of the Exchequer, announced measures in 1951 that would force people to pay half the cost of dentures and spectacles as well as a one shilling (5p post decimalisation) prescription charge, Bevan resigned from government.

While government found itself increasingly overstretched and out of its depth, attempting to do the whole job itself rather than working in partnership, the marginalisation of voluntary involvement became part of a slow but insidious slide towards the weak and passive 'it's-not-my-responsibility, it's-what-I-pay-my-taxes-for' form of democracy we now experience. Moreover, as I know myself, when I am not involved in something, it's much easier to become a negative arm-chair critic rather than a positive supporter in the ongoing battle to move things forward.

So now, with ever-growing numbers to care for and tighter and tighter budgets, we desperately need some fresh thinking. We need a genuine 'health' service – a complementary service to the NHS – which is dedicated to prevention and early engagement with people, rather than waiting until they are sick to attempt to diagnose and cure them. And, if we are to build this safety net – one that isn't full of holes and that does its job for those who are presently in free fall – the voluntary sector has a critical role too.

The latest attempt by the NHS to tackle this is the development of Integrated Care Systems (known as ICSs). But as good as the impulse is, from my experience – both of being asked to speak to the leaders of many of these new initiatives and of trying to work with them down on the ground – much more work needs to be done to engage grassroots voluntary agencies, who would be capable of adding huge amounts of capacity, innovation and real local impact.

After a decade of austerity, and the renewed struggle ahead of us, if local charities are to step up further, they need a much clearer, more authentic and mutually beneficial relationship with both local and national government – and with businesses too.

Every government has a responsibility to deliver best value to ensure that taxpayers' money is used for the greatest impact. Local charities – those close to and on the ground in the neighbourhoods they serve – not only offer all their partners a whole lot more value for money than is available elsewhere, they are already playing an increasing role as the gap between the wealthiest and the poorest becomes a chasm.

As I write, there are approximately 2,600 food banks in operation in the UK – more than all the branches of McDonald's and Starbucks combined. It's a number that continues to grow week by week. No one in the voluntary sector seeks to dominate welfare provision, but simply to play their part. Who would want a return to the old pre-National Health days? But it is the responsibility of government in its various forms, and of the statutory bodies charged with using the resources and funds at their disposal, to support projects that offer and deliver proper value for money and quality of service to ensure that they all pass the 'bang for buck' test.

Take just one example. Twelve years ago, Jo joined our church and had an idea. That Christmas, she organised us to give enough food to fill five small baskets with food for five local families in need. Over the years this initiative has grown, so that in 2022 we distributed over 100 tonnes of food to more than 12,000 people, working in partnership with around 100 businesses, other churches and faith groups, charities and organisations in our local area.

What the voluntary sector needs going forward is genuine partnership; the opportunity to sit at the decision-making table. We want to be talked with, not talked about, because we know that we have something important to bring. Genuine partnership happens when government in all its array of national and local incarnations (which of course includes the statutory organisations) begins to work in deeper and more respectful relationship with us.

The challenge is that, at the moment, talk of 'co-production' and 'co-operation' often amounts to nothing more than a 'master–servant' style reality, a relationship in which officials with little or no real delivery or community-development experience hold all the power, money and control, but none of the grassroots expertise. That doesn't make for relationship: its real name is servitude.

The combination of this breakdown in trusted relationships and short-term, uncertain government funding leaves grassroots organisations, for all their local knowledge, passion, relationships and energy, struggling to survive. Too many wonderful local charities find themselves caught in a perpetual cycle of restructuring – both up and down – which wastes cash and time, haemorrhages talent, and squanders organisational intelligence and memory.

What's more, while inequality and poverty continue to heap both reliance and demand on the whole charitable sector, they simultaneously squeeze its capacity to raise funds. It's a double whammy – funding down, need up! So, ironically, the reality is that the best equipped and so most sustainable voluntary organisations tend to be based in communities that are least impacted by poverty, and the poorest, most 'left-behind' neighbourhoods are those that are also least-well supported by local charities.

All this means that without a new understanding – a new settlement – the increasing reliance on the voluntary sector to fill the gaps that our society finds itself in, risks over-stretching it, which will only further entrench the already deep-seated inequality across the UK.

It was at the height of the Covid pandemic in June 2020, that then Prime Minister, Boris Johnson, commissioned Danny Kruger, a Conversative MP, to draw up a set of proposals around how to sustain the community spirit seen in the crisis. In response, Kruger outlined what he decided to term a 'new social covenant' as a way in which civil society could contribute to the Prime Minister's 'levelling up' agenda and so strengthen families and local communities.[9]

Kruger's definition of this social covenant was 'the mutual commitment by citizens, civil society, businesses and the state, each to fulfil their discrete responsibilities and to work together for the common good of all'. But he added, 'We need a new social and economic model to achieve this…a wholly new paradigm…in which community power replaces the dominance of remote public and private sector bureaucracies.'[10]

Does all this sound just a little reminiscent of Michael Marmot? So, now listen to some of Kruger's 'Levelling Up Our Communities' more detailed proposals:

- A 'Community Power Act' to give local people more say over the design and delivery of public services.

---

9 'Levelling Up Our Communities: proposals for a new social covenant'
10 Levelling Up Our Communities is available at https://www.dannykruger.org.uk/communities-report

- A new National Volunteer Reserve to help with future emergencies and ongoing environmental challenges.
- Paid 'service opportunities' for unemployed young people to work on social and environmental projects.
- An annual Neighbour Day bank holiday to celebrate communities and volunteering.
- A deal with faith communities to work with the public sector on big social challenges.
- A deal with Big Tech to design new 'digital infrastructure' for communities.
- And a new £500 million Community Recovery Fund to help civil society take up its developing role and a new £2 billion endowment – the 'Levelling Up Communities Fund'– for investment in long-term, community-led transformation in left-behind areas.

We have to move away from the 'economic and social doctrines which have caused us to become the most regionally unequal country in the developed world, with a range of chronic social challenges,' Kruger insisted. 'The era now opening must address these challenges by putting communities at the heart of policy making.'

But then Johnson's government fell apart – and Kruger's report went with it.

Enter – or rather re-enter – Will Tanner. Tanner, the former director of 'Onward', a think tank formed in May 2022 to help shape the 'levelling up' agenda for Boris Johnson's administration, also recognised that 'empowering local people is the key to levelling up'. Then, in November 2022, he found himself appointed as deputy chief of staff to Rishi Sunak for his spell at Number 10.

Oldham, an industrial town in Greater Manchester, had been where, earlier in the year, Tanner's 'Onward' launched its 'first-of-a-kind programme to help level up left-behind areas'. It is well known that the social fabric of industrial and coastal towns has particularly deteriorated over the last years, and that these communities face huge socio-economic challenges.

So what did Onward's 'first-of-a-kind levelling up programme for left-behind areas' get done?

Well, it turned out to be the production of yet another report! This one called 'Levelling Up In Practice'. 'If we are going to reverse decades of socio-economic decline, and restore a sense of opportunity and belonging to parts of the UK where they've been lost, we need a new partnership,' it suggested, because localism is often much better at delivering the services that people really need.[11,12] 'Oldham suffers from a lack of local pride, community, safety and cohesion,' wrote Tanner. 'To tackle these problems, Onward proposes that the relevant authorities bring local assets such as clubs and vacant shops into community ownership, bolster youth services and hire more PCSOs [Police Community Support Officers].' And because it noted that the satisfaction levels with the council and other authorities were low, Onward recommended that, 'Local leaders should find ways to increase these through better involving civil society with their decision making and expanding parish councils in the borough.'

But how can any of that be achieved without a new paradigm in partnership, and stable funding for the voluntary sector? The report didn't even ask that question, let alone suggest an answer.

Oasis works in various coastal and industrial towns, including Oldham, as well as some of the other most socio-economically disadvantaged communities around the country. In doing so, our ambition is always, in partnership with others, to develop

---

11 https://conservativehome.com/2022/02/02/will-tanner-everyone-knows-the-moral-case-for-levelling-up-but-it-makes-economic-sense-too/

12 *The Times* RED BOX, WILL TANNER – Empowering local people is the key to levelling up, Tuesday May 10 2022

working models of sustainable integrated and holistic health and wellbeing.[13]

I believe that the core principles sitting at the centre of that neighbourhood-based development work – wherever we have been able to fund it properly – hold some of the keys to better welfare, not only for children but also for whole communities, as we have demonstrated many times since Oasis was set up in 1985.

Here in the UK, Oasis currently provides schooling for some 32,500 children and young people, in fifty-two schools, as well as substantial amounts of supported housing and healthcare for vulnerable people. Our wider community work includes children's centres, sports clubs, gyms, farms, libraries, adult-learning initiatives, food banks, social supermarkets, debt and legal advice, credit unions, shops, cafes, choirs, local churches and much more; all supporting tens of thousands of children and young people, parents, carers and other community members every single day of the year.

For instance, in Waterloo, south London, aside from our primary and secondary school, we have worked hard to fund and sustain a children's centre; a children's, families and youth service; a debt, legal and relationships advice centre; a food bank; the community farm; housing for refugees; and working in partnership with our local hospital to provide a support service in an emergency centre to young people who have been victims of violent crime, as well as therapeutic support for children, parents and our staff.

It is a struggle because, in spite of the constant visits of politicians and researchers to learn from our model, the fight for sustainable funding never ends, even though positive outcomes have been achieved. For example, as a result of our work over the last ten years, we have seen a dramatic fall in local young people being

---

13 Oasis currently works in forty local neighbourhoods around the UK, and more in other countries around the world.

exploited and criminalised, and a huge rise in achievement and attainment in educational terms and life opportunities. Put bluntly, we now send more young people to Oxford, Cambridge and other Russell Group universities than used to end up in the criminal justice system before we began.

But if the internal coordination of the different parts of our work is key to this, so are the external partnerships we work hard to forge with other grassroots community organisations, charities, churches, mosques, other faith groups, businesses, the NHS, the police, social services, and of course central and local government.

It is tough work. It puts us in the muck and bullets. We face constant setbacks. But it is the future. And wherever we can muster enough resources to achieve it – as we stretch every pound as far as it will possibly go – it turns lives around.[14]

It's time to invest in doing the 'Big Society' the 'small community' way!

---

14 Wherever Oasis works our aim is always the same: to serve, respect and welcome all people regardless of their gender, race, ethnic origin, religion, age, sexual orientation or physical and mental capability, as well as to work with the whole community to create a neighbourhood in which people feel known, able to thrive and can build deep and nourishing relationships.

Principle four
Without a vision the people perish

Years back, I had a job with BBC Radio as the presenter of a series of programmes called *Changing Places*, all about people and projects working to transform local communities. As part of this, I had the opportunity to interview an Australian sheep farmer while recording in Wales. We talked about the similarities and differences in the sheep-rearing methodology of the two nations. He described how the use of fencing to keep sheep in on the enormous expanses of the Australian outback simply wasn't practical. 'So, what do you do?' I asked.

He smiled. 'We sink a well to create a supply of fresh water. The sheep will never wander too far from that well,' he explained.

The way I see it, vision is the well of fresh water in a barren desert of reports and data. It is around this well that ideas and partnerships are built and sustained, the only context in which any of the data and reports can be correctly understood or applied.

'Plans are worthless, but planning is everything,' said Dwight Eisenhower who, before becoming the President of the United States, served as Supreme Commander of the Allied Expeditionary Force in Europe during the Second World War, and planned the successful counter-invasion of North Africa in 1942–43 and Normandy in 1944–45.[15]

---

15 1958, Public Papers of the Presidents of the United States, Dwight D. Eisenhower, 1957, Containing the Public Messages, Speeches, and Statements of the President, Remarks at the National Defense Executive Reserve Conference, Date: November 14, 1957, Start Page 817, Quote Page 818, Published by the Federal Register Division, National Archives and Records Service, General Services Administration, Washington D.C.

There is more than a little wisdom in Eisenhower's seemingly paradoxical statement. No plan survives first contact with the enemy. Although some of the principles of a well-drawn battleplan may prove to be extremely helpful, once the battle begins, the inspiration of the moment also becomes front and central to survival. Put differently by former heavy weight world boxing champion Mike Tyson, 'Everybody has plans until they get hit for the first time.'

Every organisation I know, or have ever known, loves a plan. We all like developing long-range detailed strategies: three, five and ten years or more. Over the decades, however, I've come to realise that in doing so, we all make a rash assumption. An assumption is a conclusion reached prematurely, without proper assessment and which is allowed to shape our thinking. And, here is that big assumption: we assume that the future will simply be a long extension of the present. It never is. The result is that we are all chronically surprised by, and unprepared for, reality.

Do you know of any organisation that has ever fulfilled its long-term plan, as originally designed? For example, is there a company, charity or government anywhere in the world that has achieved the strategy it had for growth before the Covid pandemic hit, closely followed by Russia's invasion of Ukraine?

This is why all successful movements are guided by a strong sense of vision, rather than by plans and strategies. Strategies become blind guides if they are clung to too closely. They are too binary, too rigid. They easily become straitjackets, imprisoning an organisation instead of setting it free to achieve its real core purpose. The way I see it, what we call 'strategy' is far better understood as the 'structure' that we build around an idea once we've had it: an idea that is generated by our sense of vision. If we can find a way of creating an achievable, workable structure around it, the idea flies and becomes part of our work. If we can't, it dies or is adapted, and we move on until we find another idea, generated by our vision, that does work. Although well-developed strategies help an organisation with its planning, it's only a strong vision that will keep it relevant, effective and alive.

Vision is about where you want to go. So, whereas the various strategies you write are essential, they are, in another sense, simply descriptions of the possible roadways you are committed to building at that time, which you hope will help move you towards your destination.

We've all witnessed the gradual atrophy that can creep across even the biggest and once most powerful entities. Large, lumbering beasts, slowly dying, but taking fifty years or more to do so. No amount of money or privilege can protect them from this atrophy; only a clear sense of vision, a burning hunger to change the world, can offer immunity.

I've not known James for very long. We first met when he and I were speaking at the same event. James leads a young and brilliant community-based mentoring organisation, which works with teenagers around the development of music, recording, music management, promotion, finance and other business skills.

As James spoke, introducing the audience to some of the young people he and his organisation were mentoring, he also happened to mention that they now found themselves needing a new base for their recording studio. After the event, I managed to find him in the crowd. I introduced myself to him and told him how impressed I was with what he was doing. I also said that, if he was interested, I might be able to find a studio and office space for him. He gave me his phone number. Having done a little research, a couple of weeks later, I rang James and asked him if he was still looking for that studio and office space. He was. So, I told him that I thought I'd found something he might like and invited him to come and see it.

On the day I met with James and some of his colleagues to show them around the space we had, and could make available to them,

I asked them if they were interested. You should have seen their faces. They were ecstatic. Having sorted out some of the details together (that's when the planning bit begins), James gave me a lift back to the local railway station. On the way, he took the opportunity to quiz me about what I'd learned from the growth of Oasis over the decades. I explained that perhaps the biggest learning was that a compelling vision – rather than a fixation with writing and then chasing the fulfilment of a detailed strategy – is the only reliable guide. He looked shocked. 'But surely you also need a clear strategy,' he said.

'Put it this way,' I answered. 'Do you have a strategy?'

'Yes,' he replied.

'Great,' I said. 'And, does it contain the goal of basing yourself in this community, working with these young people, in these local schools, developing the opportunities that these particular buildings and their grounds – the ones I've just shown you – might bring? Oh, and working in partnership with me and Oasis?'

James laughed. The point was made.

Planning is essential. A vision is of little use without the practical and detailed steps to accomplish it. Any and every team needs more than inspiration. It needs information and instruction. Information to identify resources and mobilise specific members of the team for specific tasks. Instruction in what to do and when to do it in order to turn the vision into reality. However, if we are not ready to tear up those plans and strategies and instead put our faith in our sense of vision to navigate the forever changing situation and circumstances we find ourselves confronted by, failure – slow or fast – is all that awaits us.

It is one thing for a group to have talent, resources and opportunity. But it's always great vision that precedes great achievement. Any and every effective team is dependent on a compelling sense of purpose to supply it with direction. Vision is the wind in our sails, without which all we can do is drift.

I once had dinner with Pele. This great Brazilian footballer, who died at the very end of 2022, used to be the patron of Oasis' work in Brazil. More importantly, he had played football at every level possible, from schoolboy teams to his national team, and to winning the World Cup – three times! The only player ever to do so.

Pele was in London, and kindly invited me to spend the evening with him. I'll never forget our conversation. He explained to me that his experience was that before any match, at any level, in any league, the manager always presents the team with a game plan. 'We sit and discuss it,' he said. 'We are totally committed to it. But within 30 seconds or so of the start of the game, the other team has the ball, and… well, from then on it's a mix of instinct, the broad principles you can remember of the plan and teamwork, but most of all it's the vision of that goal sitting in front of you!'

There are other problems with overdependence on strategies. One of the worst of these is distraction: an extremely serious but common disease that in some cases can even prove terminal. Distraction erodes direction, and strength of vision is the only known antidote!

Distraction is subtle. For instance, budgets are, quite rightly, always a central concern. Getting them right is an essential part of the structure that has to be built around the ideas you've created to push the vision forward. And there are also the giant considerations of safeguarding, data protection, salary scales and health and safety.

So here is the thing. Slowly and subtly, in an increasingly litigious societal environment, board and management meetings become dominated by the never-ending discussion about money, fiduciary responsibilities and risk mitigation. Under the 24/7 gaze of national, local or social media, issues get lifted out of context and instant storms can blow up, often with devastating impact as compliance becomes the overriding concern and safety the watch-word. For instance, I can't count the number of times I have been part of high-level educational meetings that didn't even mention children. No one would suggest that these issues are unimportant, but as they come to dominate, they also come to distract. A perfect set of policy documents and mass corporate stupidity are often the outcomes.

Smaller charities and grassroots movements face a particularly toxic 'double dose' of this debilitating condition. As well as compliance, they are also plagued by the eternal struggle for survival. The result: a huge temptation to chase the fashionable and available funding pots, however short-sighted or ill-informed the thinking behind them might be.

Only a strong sense of vision is able to save any organisation – be it governmental, public sector, or charitable – from the deadly fate of distraction. Vision creates passion, longing and commitment in a way that policy alone never can. It is essential to the work. Without it, the very size of the task soon becomes deadly and draining, rather than life affirming. That's why the greatest risk to any organisation, at any and every level, is the loss of its original vision or purpose. In my experience, however, it is the one thing that rarely, if ever, makes it onto a board or management team's regular agenda in any meaningful way. Instead, it is too often assumed this is understood intuitively. This is seldom the case. People need constant reminders of it, as well as the opportunities to discuss it together – not just a list of words on a wall.

The year before the Covid pandemic began, I took a phone call on my mobile from a number I didn't recognise. The voice at the other end introduced themselves as a senior manager in an NHS trust. It was mid-January. 'Would you be interested in a partnership with us?' they asked. 'We have £1 million that we would like you to use to develop the kind of integrated, holistic, collaborative approach to tackling health inequalities we know Oasis has created elsewhere in one of the deprived communities in our patch.' So far, so good.

As I enquired further, the real story became clearer. It was vital that the money – the whole £1 million – was spent before 31 March, the end of the financial year. 'That's impossible,' I explained. 'It would take several years to invest that much in a way that produces sustainable results, in any community.'

'If you want it, I'm afraid that you have to spend it all in this financial year,' came the reply.

Not wanting to lose the opportunity I asked, 'Well, could we take it all now, and then spend it over the course of the next three or four years? Between now and the end of March, off the top of my head, the most we can really spend responsibly is perhaps around £30–50,000 tops. We can use that much to recruit a good project leader and administrator. Then, if we get them in time, their job, over whatever is left of this financial year, will be to get to know and listen to community members, to find out what is going on and what their concerns are, and to start talking to the other agencies already working in the neighbourhood. After that, based on the sense of vision that we develop with the people and the opportunities that present themselves, we can begin to invest and expand. But reaching that point will take us most of the next year. We can spend more of your money then. What we need to plan is a rollout over at least three years, building something together that is sustainable, locally owned, and will last beyond the end of your cash.'

There was silence. Then, 'I understand all that but, no, if you want it, you will have to spend the whole £1 million in this financial year.'

We never took up the so-called 'opportunity'. The project never happened. In fact, in my view, as I explained at the time, it would have been far more responsible to take that £1 million and burn all of it on a bonfire in an anonymous backyard somewhere. Nothing could have been more irresponsible than splashing it around a local community, wasting it on things that no one could be sure were really wanted, let alone needed; things that would promise much, but ultimately deliver little, leaving the locals more cynical about 'authority' and with an even greater lack of trust in the next idea. But the central question is: why was Oasis offered the money in the first place? The answer: because the pressure of the budgetary system meant that the main objective was to avoid the 'risk' of closing the annual accounts with an underspend, and so ensure that the budget wasn't cut for the following year.

The original vision of the NHS, the health and wellbeing of the local community, had been buried and forgotten under the weight of the system.

It's the difference between true north and magnetic north. Magnetic north varies, it moves around, it oscillates, it swings back and forth. But true north is a constant. The pull of funding pots can leave us chasing the money rather than the vision. And then there is the pull of hierarchy, position, power and autonomy. It's hard to keep marching towards true north, and so easy to end up being seduced by the safety and security of the substitutes, which we convince ourselves are almost the same thing.

Strategies can become straitjackets, but a vision sets everyone free.

When any board convenes, it is too often assumed that everyone on it remembers why they are there. But, of course, as with everything in life, we need to be constantly reminded, because anything and everything that is taken for granted in life is very easily lost.

In order for a vision to play its function of communicating your purpose and guiding every decision your organisation makes at all levels, it has to be well and regularly articulated. It cannot be taken for granted. Only this can ensure that everyone is aligned as they work together to first identify and then realise, or adapt with the required fleetness of foot, your organisation's current strategic plans and goals.

A team that embraces a unified vision becomes focused, energised, and confident. It knows where it's headed and why it's going there. But without this, various competing agendas will begin to develop and work against each other, draining energy and drive. So, for instance, have you ever noticed how some organisations and agencies have huge rates of staff and volunteer turnover? I suggest that one of the core reasons is this very issue. People work together best when they serve a compelling and well-articulated vision. In its absence they are lost and seek fulfilment and a sense of purpose elsewhere.

In the words of General Montgomery, 'Every soldier must know, before they go into battle, how the little battle they have to fight fits into the larger picture, and how the success of their fighting will influence the battle as a whole.'[16]

This, of course, means that, even though a clear vision provides direction for the whole team, it is equally important to break it down, to create smaller, individual targets to aim for. And when battalions – or in our case organisations – choose to work together around a common purpose, it becomes essential to repeat these processes together.

Why are some people and organisations more inventive, influential, pioneering and successful than others? And why are they able to keep developing? In his famous book *Start with Why* Simon Sinek says it's not about 'what' you do. What really makes the difference

---

16 Cited in 'Review of Enterprise and Management Studies', Vol. 1, No. 1, November 2013, 11 'Leadership in a desert war: Bernard Montgomery as an unusual leader', D. Weir

is 'why' you do it.[17] From Martin Luther King to Mother Teresa or the Wright brothers to Steve Jobs, Sinek says that though they were very different, they all had one thing in common: their lives and thinking were dominated by a strong sense of 'why'. He explains that continued success is about getting past knowing 'what' you do, or 'how' to do it, and onto the far more important question of 'why?' Why do we do what we do? Why do we exist?

Sinek contends that the leaders who have had the greatest influence in the world all think, act and communicate in the same way. For them it all starts and ends with 'why' – adding that this is the exact opposite of what everyone else does. His main point is this: the stronger the sense of why, the greater the sense of loyalty from staff and volunteers it will command and so the further you will get together. Or, to quote Friedrich Nietzsche, 'Those who have a why to live for can bear almost any how.'[18]

Operating viably or profitably isn't a why. It is simply a 'what'. Instead, your why is all about your purpose. Why does your organisation exist? Why do you get out of bed in the morning? Why do you fight for what you are doing? The 'hows' and the 'whats' are obviously important, but when they come to dominate, the why gets neglected and sometimes even lost altogether, and then the 'hows' and 'whats' start to collapse.

Your 'why' grows into your vision – the cornerstone on which all else is built. The rest should never be more than simply the current description of 'how' the organisation will achieve that goal.

Under the microscope of Sinek's analysis, the thinking behind the offer that was made to me of £1 million, if spent within months,

---

17 Simon Sinek, *Start with Why: How Great Leaders Inspire Everyone to Take Action* (Portfolio, 2009).

18 In 1889 Friedrich Nietzsche published *Götzen-Dämmerung; oder, Wie man mit dem Hammer philosophiert* (*Twilight of the Idols, or, How to philosophize with a hammer*), which included a section called 'Sprüche und Pfeile' ('Maxims and Arrows').

is easy to understand. Instead of being driven by the 'why' of the NHS mission, followed up with some clear thinking around how and lastly what, it arose entirely the other way around. 'What' are we going to do with that money before 1 April to ensure that we don't end up with an awkward underspend and then get next year's budget cut? And then, 'how' will we do it? We'll ring Steve Chalke. We know him! The 'why' of their being stewards of this resource never even surfaced. But, equally, if I had accepted the £1 million, I would have let go of our 'why' in the process.

A clear sense of 'why', a clarity of vision, sets an organisation or movement's direction of travel: its true north. In other words, if you get stuck in the details, step back until you can see the big picture – the whole vision – again. Only that will keep you on track. This is the greatest and the only protection against losing it along the way. When we don't know where we're headed we meander at best. Put differently, when you have no vision, any strategy will do.

I'm a dual-heritage, south London boy. My father was a very dark-skinned Indian, trying to eke out a living in the very white culture of the 1950s to 1970s. Growing up, that meant I knew what racial discrimination felt like, first hand. Because of his colour, my father struggled to find the kind of skilled work for which he was both capable and qualified. To cut a long story short, because of my colour I was often ridiculed, added to which, and maybe because of which, I went on to fail the eleven-plus exam. As a result, I found myself in one of the worst secondary schools in the area which hardly made life easier. 'Is there any point to my life?' was my big question. To which I really did feel the answer was no.

Then, at the age of fourteen, I joined a Friday night youth club in a local church hall entirely staffed by students from the local college. And as I'd got to know them, I somehow absorbed their message. It was very different: 'Your life has huge potential – don't waste it.'

I liked their message, and even more their attitude. They noticed me. They were interested in me. They listened to me. They invested in me.

So it was that one Friday night on my way home from that church hall, I decided my mission in life would be to offer to others what they had offered to me: time, attention and a sense of purpose. And it came to me that when I grew up, I would set up a school for kids who had been starved of hope, a house that would provide security for young people who had been denied love, and some health assistance that would lavish care, kindness and support on all in their greatest moments of need or times of crisis.[19]

I should also say that I had little or no understanding of what any of this really meant, but I did know that it was what I should spend my life doing. The view I had of my life as an irrelevance had been swept away and I'd been given the gift of purpose.

Over time, my big 'why' became Oasis' big 'why', the meaning-giving story that frames our identity and from which grew the vision of Oasis: education, healthcare, housing, inclusion, equality and justice. A vision bathed in a belief that the health of our bodies, minds and spirits is all inter-linked, and an intuitive understanding that together these ingredients, when delivered freely with a love, care and attention that serves all, regardless of colour, or any other form of discrimination, creates community, hope and purpose.

It's our true north. It's our guiding star. It's our greatest asset!

---

19 To date, we have only opened one hospital, known as GM Priya in the Latur district in Maharashtra, India. However, because at that stage the work of Oasis in India was only a few years old, it was decided to give the completed hospital to the Emmanuel Hospital Association. The GM Priya hospital has subsequently grown and now specialises in AIDS and cancer care as well as neurological diseases and chronic illnesses. Although Oasis has not built any other hospitals, it is now engaged in a variety of healthcare initiatives both in the UK and beyond.

Principle five

You can judge the wisdom of any society by the investment it makes in its children

I want to tell you a story. Not one that I'm proud of. My only excuse was ignorance.

It was back in the 1980s. My wife and I, with a lot of help from friends, had just set up a safe house to provide accommodation for young people who had been rejected or exploited by those who should have loved and cared for them. It was the first outworking of the vision I had received that Friday evening, walking home through south London: to set up a house that would provide security for young people who had been denied love and hope. In fact, it was where Oasis got its name from. My wife suggested we call the house Oasis because it would be a place of sanctuary, a place of hope, a place of refreshment for all those who lived there.

But as the house filled with seventeen-, eighteen- and nineteen-year-olds, I was in for a shock. There was rarely a 'please', a 'thank you', a smile or even eye contact from any of our residents.

And that's not all. To help make the house a home, we'd kitted it out with wonderful artwork and a huge TV in the lounge. Yet, soon after our first residents arrived, everything disappeared. All stolen and sold by the very young people we had worked so hard to create an oasis for!

I was angry. What was wrong with these people?

The problem, however, as I slowly realised, was mine not theirs.

I am ashamed to admit it, but because the profound disabilities of these young people were psychological rather than physical, it was all too easy to misread their behaviours and as a result blame them rather than compensate for them. Having never stood in the ill-fitting shoes of those I sought so naively to support, the jump to my misconceived conclusions was as simple as it was misguided.

If those wounds had been broken or disfigured limbs, I would have readily compensated for them. But because they were psychological, emotional and internal, born of neglect, abandonment, fear and rejection, at first I didn't recognise them at all. And even when I did, because I'd now provided these 'lucky young people' with a room and a bed, I expected them to be able to 'just get over it'. I didn't understand how trauma disorganises the mind, creating wounds that do not heal easily.

These were the days before trauma was even talked about, before neuroscience was recognised as a discipline, before the Magnetic Resonance Imaging (MRI) scanner allowed us to see live pictures of the damage caused to a child who has been starved of the protections so many of us take for granted. But it was in this house, with these young people, that I learned perhaps the deepest truth about effective community development and the care of children, young people and their families that I know.[20] You can't divorce the external from the internal journey. Hope has to be born and built in a human heart as well as a community. In short, we need a far more therapeutically informed and transformed approach to human development sitting at the centre of every part of our social policy.

---

20 For more on this I recommend reading a good psychology book, for example, one of Dr Tina Payne Bryson and Dan Siegel's bestsellers, *The Whole-Brain Child*, *No-Drama Discipline* or *The Yes Brain*.

Today, neuroscience – the study of the human brain and its development – is the new science. And though it is still in its infancy, the impact of what we are discovering is huge. To believe that it is possible to develop social policy that protects and nurtures all children and young people without developing a new and central focus on what this truth means for our educational, social care, healthcare, mental health, policing and youth justice systems, is simply naive. It is not only to use our limited resources unwisely but, more than that, to continue to add to rather than soothe the trauma of huge numbers of children and older people in our society, through the very systems that should be helping them.

Back in the 1950s, research began to highlight the need for young children to enjoy a secure emotional bond with their primary caregiver as a vital part of their development. Known as attachment theory, this understanding was first developed by John Bowlby, a British psychologist, psychiatrist, and psychoanalyst. This attachment, he said, creates a base from which to explore the world and begin to form other relationships, and the quality of it affects a child's psychological, behavioural and emotional development.[21]

Then came the MRI revolution. The first MRI scanner to be put into clinical use anywhere in the world was introduced by the NHS into Aberdeen Royal Infirmary in 1981, but it was not until the 1990s that they became widely available, opening up huge new opportunities for understanding the human brain and its development.

I remember so well the first time I was shown MRI images of the brains of a group of three-year-old children. The difference between the shape and formation of the brain of a child who

---

21 Bowlby's theory of attachment suggests that children are born biologically pre-programmed to form attachments with others, because this will help them to survive. A child has an innate need to attach to one main primary caregiver. This attachment serves to keep the infant close to their mother, thus improving the child's chances of survival. Bowlby called this attachment 'monotropy', and believed that the earliest bonds formed by children with their primary caregiver and in time a small group of others has a tremendous impact that continues throughout life.

had received consistent love and one-to-one attention, time and understanding, compared to that of a child who had been abused, neglected or ignored was stark. I could literally see the difference in size and development.

Over the last thirty years, we have learned more about how the human brain works than we did through the rest of human history. It may show up as depression, anxiety, anger, failed relationships, or addictions to everything from gambling or shopping to substance abuse, self-harm, sex, violence, alcohol, food, violence or anything else. However, all these are only ever the symptoms of the problem. The real issue is the pain caused by the deep wounds of the past for which healing has never been found. That's why it's time to change our approach to health and mental health. But still today, the role that trauma and developmental adversity play in a person's mental health remains vastly underappreciated.

In the eighteenth century, the treatment of patients with mental health disorders was barbaric. Bleeding, forced vomiting, cold baths, debilitating drugs, the use of cages, whips and chains were all administered in the attempt to weaken the 'animal spirit' which was believed to be producing madness.

Lunatics, as they were called, had lost their power of reason, which was considered by many at the time to be the very essence of what it was to be human. Only these brutal treatments might put things right for them. 'Madness' was the consequence of allowing your 'passions and appetites' to dethrone your reason. It was hoped that the living hell of being sentenced to the asylum would serve as a warning to others to keep well away from the dangers of immorality and vice.

But the tragedy is this: two hundred and fifty years later, although we'd say we've long moved on from the worst excesses of this flawed and deeply hypocritical 'moralising', its remnants are still all too evident in our society. 'Good' people – good children – are thought to be 'good' because they control their behaviour and act in socially appropriate and morally responsible ways. On the other hand, 'bad' people are thought to be 'bad' because they display antisocial behaviours and make morally bankrupt choices. Sadly, it's with this outdated and scientifically discredited approach to morality that we remain stuck; not only in our thinking, but in terms of too many of the assumptions and implications of major aspects of our policy making.

In evolutionary terms, we now know that the brain stem is the human brain's most primitive part. Often known as the instinctual or reptilian brain, it's responsible for the most basic functions of life such as breathing and movement – the involuntary bodily processes necessary for survival. Above it is the limbic system, part of what is sometimes known as the forebrain – the emotional or feeling brain. It serves as the brain's emotional motor system and its task is to process and collate input from all our sensory systems: vision, touch, hearing, taste and smell. But, the highest level brain, the cortex, is also often known as the rational or thinking brain. It's the outer wrinkled covering of the surface of your brain and is involved in all its higher processes including learning, interpretation and problem solving.

What is known as the prefrontal cortex is located at the very front of the cortex, behind the forehead, and is responsible for our ability to manage and moderate our responses to news of all the external stimuli and events that it receives from the brain stem and limbic system. Its task is to keep us calm by processing, reflecting and reasoning; to recognise future consequences of current actions, to determine what is wise and unwise, to evaluate better and best responses, and to plan towards defined goals. In short, the cortex's job is to provide us with social control.

By the time a typical person is an adult, their prefrontal cortex takes up nearly a third of this outer layer of the brain. But the critical factor is this. None of us are born with a fully developed prefrontal cortex. The brain develops in a kind of back-to-front pattern: from the bottom up and from the inside out, and the prefrontal cortex is the last part to develop fully in this process.

This doesn't mean that children and adolescents don't have some functional prefrontal cortex, but it does mean that they won't have all the complex decision-making and planning skills adults have until they are older. In fact, most neurologists agree that the prefrontal cortex is not fully developed until around the age of twenty-five.

However, much of this critical brain development will take place before we reach the age of five. That means the quality of an infant's primary caregiving relationships, as John Bowlby said, is the foundation, not only for their future health and mental health, but also for their capacity for all future relationships. The ability to build healthy relationships throughout life lies in the gift of a few safe and stable ones in infancy. When a young child grows up in a household where love and attention are rare or sporadic, that child's future capacity for building strong, lasting and intimate relationships is stunted.

A child who experiences strong and secure attachments with their primary caregivers, as well as close relationships with extended family members and other significant carers, is far more likely to become an adult whose prefrontal cortex is well developed and therefore able to control their emotions and impulses, and to behave 'pro-socially'. This is known as self-regulation. However, just as it can be developed, it can also be stunted. Anxiety, embarrassment, fear, distress and trauma, including the impact of poverty, homelessness, violence, rejection, abuse and neglect, are very likely to inhibit the growth of essential parts of the thinking brain and disrupt development.

All this begins with a mother before the birth of her child; with her living conditions, sense of worth, security and peace, or lack of it. The stress she feels is toxic. It negatively impacts her health and therefore that of her unborn child. And, if this mother feels judged or criticised by the professionals who are there to support her, her toxic load is increased.

We now know that all incoming sensory information to the brain is processed from the bottom up. First by its lower, more primitive and reactive areas, and then by the thinking prefrontal cortex. Everything that we experience in the present moment gets filtered by the lower parts of our brain, where it is reacted to in comparison with memories of previous similar experiences, before even getting anywhere near our cortex. That means that a person who has endured a life of chaos, with extreme and prolonged stress, particularly in the first years of their life, is more likely to act without thought for the consequences of their behaviour.

Behaviours that stem from reactions to these adverse experiences of early childhood often have a long fuse. They can be like time bombs. Small children are not big enough or strong enough to intervene in the violence they witness. So, for example, they simply watch their father beat their mother, and internalise the impact of what they have experienced. That takes its toll and may well have repercussions throughout later life. Thus, the behaviour that we see in an angry, aggressive teenager is often inextricably linked to the violence that they witnessed as a three-year-old child. Study after study tells us the same thing. The care and protection extended to or withheld from a child has long-term repercussions. When circumstances provoke an association, whether conscious or subconscious, violence can become just one of the destructive ways of responding to those memories.

A child or young person with a limbic system that has become highly sensitised by continuous stress can experience an overload and a temporary shutdown of their prefrontal cortex. And once this happens, they are at the mercy of their dysregulated limbic system. They are simply unable to cope, to cool down and self-regulate. Traumatised children and young people can have extremely severe reactions to particular places, situations, activities, sounds, or people which trigger flashbacks to terrible memories, and often sudden negative emotional mood swings or even physical responses.

At this point, the person may have very poor access to any social method of problem solving or to high-level cognitive processes such as the ability to rationalise. Their preoccupation is survival. Energy preservation demands that engagement is focused only on those activities that guarantee safety. They often also become individualistic, with a diminished capacity to empathise or cooperate. They have little room to think about anybody else's needs. And, if they cannot find a legitimate way to regulate their tension or stress, then they may have no choice but to discharge it, often – though not always – through explosive aggression or violence, either to others or to themselves.

Some young people refer to losing control in this kind of uninhibited way as 'switching'. But, although the resulting aggression and violence is distressing for them and for those around them, anything that enables them to escape from the nightmare that has taken over their brain is cathartic. The violence has the same impact as the release of steam from a pressure cooker. It restores equilibrium and the exhaustion that follows brings temporary peace. Even the attempt to take your own life can be a way of managing emotions.

The old-world, binary thinking around morality would describe these dysregulated and traumatised children, young people and adults as selfish and morally flawed. It is too easy to assume, for instance, that all violence is a selfish, immoral, outrageous act of personal power and defiance, and that punishment is the most meaningful way to correct the problem.

The reality is that these children are almost all victims of circumstance who have 'appropriately' adapted to the dysfunctional world they have been forced to endure. They don't decide to explode, but their capacity to manage their emotions is limited. Something triggers them and they are spun out of control. Only after the whirlwind has passed can they regain a sense of conscious awareness and realise the gravity of the thing they have done.

Our assumption is that children are born with resilience built in. 'Don't worry. They will be OK. They will bounce back. They'll be fine, they are only young. They'll get over it', we say. But it's not true. Children are not resilient.

If you squeeze a sponge and then let go, it will spring back into shape. Resilience is that elastic bounce-back quality. But a child's brain is only just being built through the experiences they are encountering. It's plastic, not elastic. It's like plasticine: shapable, mouldable, suggestible, impressionable, which means that through abuse, violence or neglect, it will easily become misshaped. That is not to say that children, just like adults, can't demonstrate resilience, but only after they have been shaped rather than misshaped. The impact of trauma doesn't simply fade away. Unless and until our policies and practice both acknowledge and respond to this fact, there will be no healing.

When a child is stressed, there is a graded response, gradually activating the systems in the brain and body designed to help them survive: from calm, to alert, to alarm, to fear, to terror. When the most regulated adult is not under stress, they can be calm, using their time and thinking power productively. However, as soon as they face a challenge (lose their phone, misplace their car keys, or find themselves running late for an important meeting or deadline) they enter a state of alarm – just when they most need it, their sense of equilibrium deserts them. This all happens because deep in the brain, clusters of neurons play a vital part in our development. A fully grown adult has almost 100 billion brain cells, or neurons, which form pathways. A neural pathway is a string of connected neurons that sends signals from one part of the brain to another;

for instance, from our limbic system to our prefrontal cortex. This pathway is established through continual use in just the same way as a physical track is formed across a field. Given behaviours in response to specific stimuli become habits and the neutral pathways formed eventually become the brain's autobahns.

If, since childhood, you've come to associate chocolate with comfort, reward and feeling good when you need an emotional lift, you will automatically take the path, physically as well as psychologically, to that box of chocolates. And every time you do it, that pathway is reinforced. (By the way, this is why, although a diet will help you lose weight in the short term, unless you change those pathways your weight loss will never be sustainable.) Or, take another example, if a baby smiles and is rewarded with a kiss and a cuddle, a neural pathway begins to form. If a young child touches something sharp and it hurts, a neural pathway begins to be laid down. But not all experiences are beneficial. A young child who has witnessed domestic violence may develop neural pathways which lead them to feel fear and withdraw from situations involving confrontation. A girl who is sexually abused by a man may shut down emotionally and not let any man near her. Or she may begin to find ways of deliberately hurting anyone who gets too close to her.

The good news is that just like a real road system, however well-worn that pathway has become there is the potential for it to be changed or adapted. Hope is always real. The brain is ever-changing. And, although our brains develop new neural pathways much faster in childhood and our early teen years than at any other point, they keep doing it throughout our lives. This means that new pathways and new habits can always be forged. This flexibility is known as neuroplasticity and it's how some people who have had strokes are able to retrain themselves to speak or walk again. And it's this that enables even the most traumatised child, with the right support, training and effort, to overcome habits that once seemed unbreakable.

Of course, it is also true that no two people are the same. Not all traumatised children or adults will react in the same way. In fact, we know that every brain is unique, which means that we will all experience stress, distress and trauma differently. Two people who experience exactly the same traumatic event may respond very differently to it. For instance, someone may well have poor brain development, brain damage or a brain injury that causes them to display aggressive and destructive behaviour. Someone else, whose prefrontal cortex has also not developed well, may instead be incapable of being socially responsive to his or her child.

So, if you've been wound up by someone taking a long time to get on or off the bus when you are in a hurry, but have been able to refrain from exploding by thinking through the reasons why this has happened, you owe it to your prefrontal cortex. It has managed to cool your limbic system down and successfully self-regulated your response. But if, on occasion, your prefrontal cortex is unable to control your heated-up limbic system, that's when you have a tantrum: you shout or throw something, behave aggressively or are intolerant.

The truth is that as we lose access to the higher part of our brain, our thinking and behaviour starts to be driven by our more primitive, reactive limbic centre. As I have learned over the years, the more stressed I am, the more stupidly I behave! That's it. None of this is 'them' and 'us'. We have all had a childhood. As a friend of mine puts it: that's why we need to choose our parents wisely! On top of all this, the latest research into what is known as epigenetics is helping us understand that some people appear to have a greater, genetically influenced capacity for emotional and social resilience, while others have a far more sensitive stress response and are much more easily overwhelmed.

The study of epigenetics is still at an early stage, but we are now beginning to understand that the experiences of our grandparents, great grandparents and ancestors even further back can have a significant ongoing influence on our experience of life. We know that childhood trauma can alter our gene activity. It can turn them on or off as they adapt with the aim of improving our short-term survival in an adverse and hostile environment. Genes have a 'memory', and studies, for instance, of the offspring of children evacuated during the Second World War, the Vietnam and Iraq wars, the survivors of the Holocaust and the Romanian orphanages, suggest that in some cases these epigenetic changes can be stored in the egg or sperm and then passed on to future generations.

Some of this can, of course, be explained by the impact of these experiences on the subsequent parenting styles of those who experienced them, but the experts now tell us that epigenetic alterations are also inherited. And though originally they took place to assist survival in a persistently hyper-sensitising stressful situation, over the generations these once helpful adaptive changes can become problematic or maladaptive and mean that some children are born wired for chaos, which can leave those affected with greater difficulty controlling their responses to, and recovering from, stressors. This, of course, can have an impact on their brain development, their cognition, their behaviour and health.

At the same time, it is important to remind ourselves that because the brain remains malleable throughout life, epigenetic mechanisms that regulate genes therefore have the potential for change. That's their purpose: to adapt to the environment. Though, that said, we are only just at the beginning of learning about the length of time and the therapeutic care that it takes to achieve this. All this explains why to judge every child by the same measure is to make a huge and potentially life-limiting error, which means that some of the systems supposedly developed and designed to serve these children and young people, and their families, are just not fit for purpose.

The term Adverse Childhood Experiences (ACEs) was first coined in 1995, and since then there have been an increasing number of studies identifying the long-term impacts that ACEs can have on health throughout life. ACEs refer to the sources of stress that a child may suffer while growing up, such as sexual, physical or emotional abuse; neglect; exposure to domestic violence; parental substance abuse; mental illness or separation, and so on. These have both immediate and life-long impacts, dramatically increasing the risk of future poor psychological health. While many people who have experienced ACEs are resilient to their harmful effects, for others, ACEs can have long-lasting impacts.

Childhood trauma is also much more common than you might think. Research by Public Health Wales in 2015, with a cross section of people aged eighteen to sixty-five, revealed that almost half (47%) of those interviewed reported at least one ACE. But 14% reported four or more. More than that, compared with participants who reported no ACEs, those with four and over were four times more likely to be high-risk drinkers; fifteen times more likely to have committed violence in the previous twelve months; sixteen times more likely to have used crack cocaine or heroin; and twenty times more likely to have been in prison at some point in their lives.

Importantly, we also know that children who suffer one type of ACE are at increased risk of suffering other types of ACEs, thus reflecting a need to address the causes of ACEs collectively rather than only focusing on individual adversities. Multiple ACE studies have ensued, all confirming similar statistics. In 2017 'The effect of multiple adverse childhood experiences on health', published in *The Lancet*, reported that ACEs are implicated in over 80% of all cases of children identified as being in need. Meanwhile, in May 2021, Manchester Metropolitan University's 'Serious Youth Violence and its Relationship with Adverse Childhood Experiences' report found that across the city 66% of all young people involved in the criminal justice system had five or more ACEs and 22% had eight or more. Only two young people had none.[22]

---

22 I would suggest, however, that these two may well have had either ACEs that were not uncovered or issues that were not identified as ACEs.

Studies into ACEs consistently show that the higher the number a child has been exposed to, the greater the risks relating to their education (increasing the likelihood of school absence, low engagement and low achievement), to their development of health-harming behaviours and poor mental health, and to their involvement in violence and the criminal justice systems (including the likelihood of offending).

However, it's also important to understand that treating ACEs as if they are simply additive – that two are more disturbing than one, that four are more traumatic than three and so on – is too simplistic. Every individual responds differently to their environment and may also be differently placed in terms of accessing sources of help and support. Therefore, while a single ACE might have a devastating and lifelong impact on one child, another may be more equipped to cope better in the face of several.

That said, research does reveal consistently that the more ACEs, the more likely a person is to develop risky health behaviours such as alcohol and drug misuse, multiple sexual partners, self-harm and poor eating habits, which, of course, lower their life expectancy and heighten the occurrence of conditions such as cancer, heart disease, stroke, emphysema and diabetes, as well as the health and development of offspring. On top of this devastating cost to individuals and families, the financial cost of ACEs to society, our services and systems is also vast.

This is why the growing understanding around what is often labelled as trauma-informed practice – work around the prevention and mitigation of ACEs – is so important. What is vital now is that this learning is taken on board in our future thinking around the development of social policy, including health, social care, education, policing and criminal justice, as well as the funding and practice of community development work. A genuine commitment to the introduction of trauma-informed approaches will lead to huge cost savings as well as health and wellbeing benefits.

This, of course, is one of the reasons why developing policies, legislation and strategies that promote the wider determinants of health and human rights is such a priority. Common sense tells us that inequality and poverty act as drivers of the behaviours and environments in which ACEs occur, and that anything and everything we can do to support parents and caregivers to enable safe, stable and nurturing relationships for children will create a safer society for us all.

Much has been written about what psychologists call 'fundamental attribution error'. It's a fascinating human trait. We tend to attribute our shortcomings to our circumstances: 'I was tired', 'I'd had a tough day', 'They don't know what I'm trying to deal with right now', and so on. But, when it comes to others, we're prone to ignore all this, convinced that unlike us they do bad things simply because they are bad people! What they do reflects who they are, whereas what we do is simply a result of what has happened to us and the stress that we are under.[23]

Have you ever seen the experiment with fleas? You can watch it on YouTube.[24] When a flea is caught and placed in a jar and the lid is put on, the flea will jump, over and over again, hitting its head on that lid for several days. Every flea is capable of jumping several times higher than the lid of any jar. However, eventually the flea will learn and adapt its behaviour. From that point on, whenever the flea jumps, it will always jump just a little short of the height of the top of the jar. It will never hit its head again. It will avoid the pain. And, surprisingly, when the lid is removed, the flea will still not jump beyond the height of the lid. It has learnt. Its behaviour is set. It has created an imaginary lid for itself which it will never try to break through. It will never attempt to jump beyond the height of the lid again in its lifetime. And, astonishingly, nor will

---

23 For more on fundamental attribution error, see: https://ethicsunwrapped.utexas.edu/glossary/fundamental-attribution-error.

24 View at: https://www.youtube.com/watch?v=bjmfaZyNvDg, or simply type 'jumping fleas and the jar' into your search engine.

its offspring, or their offspring. The non-existent lid has become the defining factor in their lives, the story that controls their future.

In their book, *What Happened to You?*, Dr Bruce Perry and Oprah Winfrey illustrate this by talking about the fear of dogs. This is sometimes based on the personal experience of being bitten by a dog, which creates an association and therefore a real sense of threat from all dogs, however small and unthreatening to others they might be. But some people are terrified of dogs even though they've never been bitten or even growled at by one. Their fear is what we now understand as 'trans-generationally transmitted'. How does this happen? Well, for instance, a child will sense and feel fear around a dog if their parent, who once was chased by a dog, squeezes their hand harder as someone with a dog passes, or avoids the situation altogether by crossing the street as soon as they see the 'threat' coming. But, of course, the fear of the parent may have been transmitted to them in just the same way.[25]

What happened to us influences who we become in complex ways. However, it's not just our direct experiences, or even what we inherit and absorb from previous generations of our family. It is also an outcome of the way that wider society and the culture we are part of works around us.

This means that if we are going to make real progress in our support of individual children and families at a micro level, we've also got to recognise and grapple with the fact that trauma-creating bias takes place at whole-community and societal levels. If a system is truly trauma informed, for instance, it will also be anti-racist. Which is why the fight against racism, Islamophobia, homophobia, transphobia, gender inequality and the marginalisation of other people groups, along with the recognition of neurodiversity and the impact of disability, is so important. That's also why the reform

---

25 Bruce Perry and Oprah Winfrey, *What Happened to You? Conversations on trauma, resilience, and healing* (Colorado: Bluebird, 2021).

of all our welfare and social systems is essential, as we work to bring to an end policies and methods of working which either implicitly or explicitly carry with them prejudices and biases, or the seeds of family or community fragmentation.

And as Oprah says in that same book, *What Happened to You?*, 'everything matters'. Everything that has ever happened to you, to your parents, to their parents before them, along with your experience of community and the wider culture and society that you find yourself part of, it all matters – everything!

Principle six
Individually we are one drop; together we are an ocean

Early this very morning I listened to the news headlines on national radio. The top story explored the crisis around the fact that nearly 40% of nineteen- to twenty-one-year-olds who have spent time in care as children are now not in education, employment or training, compared with around 11% of all people of the same age across England. The last line of the report was this official government response: 'The government says there is a £1,000 bursary and provision of practical support to help care leavers aged between sixteen and twenty-four to live independently.'

Of course, money is important, but it's also time that our funding regimes caught up with the science, all that we now know about childhood development and the power of community. This means that if the best we have to offer is writing another cheque, we are sunk. What we really need is an overarching, inclusive, joined-up, child-first vision and then a long-term thoughtful plan that implements it.

A few years ago, I hosted a debate with a senior politician – a cabinet member – around the policies his department was responsible for. Taking questions from the floor, he was asked, 'If you understand so clearly what's wrong, then why don't you change it?' I'll never forget his response. 'You don't understand,' he said. 'What can I do?' The audience laughed, mostly out of their sense of shock. But I understood what he meant. We've inherited a system where almost everyone feels impotent and powerless. But, it needn't be that way.

Way back in the long hot summer of 1858, the stench from the River Thames terrified Londoners. The 'Great Stink' as they called it, the smell of raw sewage in the river, was so strong that it even caused parliament to close.

A few years earlier there had been several terrible outbreaks of cholera in which tens of thousands of people died. As a response to this, John Snow, a London-based physician, published a paper, 'On the Mode of Communication of Cholera', in which he proposed that cholera was not transmitted, as was the popular belief, by bad smelly air but instead by waterborne infection. However, he had struggled to convince the wider medical establishment of his theory.

Over the decades, the Thames had effectively become London's largest open sewer: a problem that had also been exacerbated by the recent invention of the water closet. This meant that huge amounts of sewage were being flushed straight into the river every day and, because of the ebb and flow of the tide, were just sitting there warming in the summer sun. The cover of *Punch* magazine for 10 July 1858 had a cartoon of what it called the Silent Highwayman (death), in a boat on the river and the simple caption, 'Your Money or your Life!'

In response, still committed to the belief that 'all bad smell is disease', parliament decided to sanction one of the century's great engineering projects: a new sewer network for London to carry the smell away from the city.

Joseph Bazalgette, the famous engineer, was appointed by government and given the task of building a network of new sewers to intercept the waste and help ensure there were no further cholera outbreaks caused by 'bad air'. The new sewerage system was finally opened in 1865, just before cholera returned for one final time in 1866. However, the victims of this outbreak were almost entirely confined to the slums of east London, which had not yet been connected to the new sewers, leaving them with little option but to drink contaminated water. This final outbreak at last provided conclusive evidence that Snow's theory of the waterborne transmission of cholera was correct. The outcome of which was that the 'bad air' theory of disease transmission was abandoned and sewerage systems began to be built around the world. It's time once more to catch up with the science!

In the previous chapter we talked about trauma. Trauma runs through generations, across families, communities, institutions, cultures and whole societies. It impacts our health, thinking, feeling, behaving, parenting and relationships and none of this will change until we find the will to change our systems. To that end, it's time for us to commit to a number of honest, grown-up conversations about the quality and consistency of our systems and about the way they integrate with each other, in the light of our developing scientific understanding and concern for public health. Let's start with education. However, as you will see, we can't stop there...

When a child is excluded from school, their sense of rejection is deep. However, our national school system is not designed for the child with special educational needs. Instead, it acts like a straitjacket: every child is expected to fit into the 'norm'. Their 'success' is judged by our limitations, rather than by an understanding of their situation or potential. In other words, the system we operate punishes a child because of who they are and what has happened to them. It's crazy.

A child with traumatic experiences will often have difficulty learning and is also likely to be overreactive to the feedback and criticisms that come with struggling in school. This, of course, will lead to further behavioural issues, which will also be misunderstood.

Take primary school, with the challenge of meeting a teacher and making new friends. What may seem to be a moderate, developmentally appropriate challenge for most children may be overwhelming for others. Think about the five-year-old who only has the language skills, or the self-regulation capacity, of the typical three-year-old along with the overreactive stress response that goes with it. This is the start of a toxic mismatch between the child's capabilities and the unrealistic expectations of an education system. Note I say system rather than school. It is that that's largely under-resourced, neuro-unaware, developmentally uninformed and trauma ignorant.

Then there's the huge change from primary school and the familiarity of 'my desk', 'my coat peg', 'my teacher', and 'my friends' into the completely new environment of secondary school where everything is much bigger, unfamiliar and most of the rules have changed. What happens when this same child enters this new school environment with all its different customs and expectations, rules and curriculum design? The school, of course, is geared up and funded for this child to act typically. The problem is that this will be impossible, and levels of frustration will grow for the child, for their classmates and, of course, for their teachers.

Soon letters of complaint will be arriving from other parents, with threats of removing their children from the school. How does the school respond to this situation? How do they deal with the financial threat of a number of parents acting on their promise and removing their children? What will be the impact of that on the school budget? The only way forward is to sanction the child, in an attempt to push them into compliance. But in this overwhelmingly distressing situation, the child in question will either retreat inside themselves (dissociate) or explode. Either way, they will not be receiving the social, emotional or academic learning they need.

So, they fall further behind.

When a child is physically ill, we all instantly understand why they can't be in school. But, those who struggle with poor mental health and undiagnosed special educational needs too often end up being wrongly labelled as 'school refusers', instead of what they actually are: children with debilitating levels of anxiety and a crippling loss of confidence. So when they try to avoid the constant humiliation of school, they are charged with truancy. But when they are in school, they will be given detentions and demerits, sent to internal inclusion units, issued with fixed-term exclusions, and may eventually even be permanently excluded.

But exclusion solves nothing; instead it does the opposite: it deepens the problem. It labels the child as 'bad'. And, on top of all else, this simply reinforces their existing belief that they're just not good enough. Of course, a child who is struggling is not going to say that their teachers don't understand them or admit that they don't understand themselves. So, they simply conclude that they are misfits and learn to wear that label. And all that does is add to their trauma.

A story. No one knew that the new boy in town and at the school had been sexually abused regularly by his uncle every time he stayed at the old family home over a period of the previous three years. No one knew that this was why his brain had come to associate various adult male attributes with panic and fear – or that his new teacher physically fitted the bill.

So when the boy became defensive, aggressive, and unresponsive to the teacher's efforts to engage with him, his teacher had no idea why this was happening. A few days in, this bright and caring young teacher decided to walk over to the boy, help him with some work and break through the barrier that he could clearly sense. But as he bent down to the desk, his eyes met the boy's. The child was triggered. He snapped. His prefrontal cortex had been overloaded: his lower brain had taken over. He lashed out. Later on, once he was calm, the boy agreed that his behaviour was wrong. But, although he couldn't even begin to explain it, in the moment that it happened he had no access to reason.

His brain's fight or flight stress response had been triggered by his past experience of his uncle, and he simply responded accordingly.

His teacher didn't understand it, the school didn't understand it. His parents didn't understand it, and nor did the boy. But from then on everyone, including the boy, regarded him as a problem, even though in view of his past, his response had been totally predictable.

Our schools need the resources and support to enable their staff to develop the skills to deal with the prevalence of childhood adversity and its impact on learning, along with the strategies to create regulated, safe and secure classrooms.

The now famous phrase 'It's not what's wrong with you, it's what happened to you' originated with Dr Sandra Bloom and Joseph Foderaro, in the early 1990s, as part of a conversation around their work with adult patients with serious mental health issues. 'It's that we've changed the fundamental question from "What's wrong with you?" to "What happened to you?"' Joe explained to Sandra one day. The phrase stuck, but thirty years later it's time that the practice did too.[26]

It's also worth noting that a truly trauma-informed system takes the same approach to its staff as it does to its clients – in the case of a school, to its children. Trauma at the top of any system always gets passed down through that system. From the regulators to the senior staff, to the junior staff, and onto the children and young

---

26 In Dr Sandra Bloom's book *Creating Sanctuary: Toward the evolution of sane societies* (Routledge, 1997), the discovery of 'It's not what's wrong with you, but what happened to you' is explained on page 191 in this way: 'Our program director [Joe Federaro] said it best when he observed that we [the Sanctuary program] had stopped asking the fundamental question "What's wrong with you?' and changed it to "What has happened to you?"' The book is a description of a hospital-based programme to treat adults who had been abused as children and the revolution in their care that this simple but profound principle created. Fifteen years later, Sandra Bloom updated her book which now includes new material on Adverse Childhood Experiences, epigenetics, and what we now know about the brain and violence.

people it is supposedly set up to serve. Everyone gets traumatised. Which, of course, is the major reason, by far, that there is such a high turnover of staff in so many of the caring services. Currently, some 40% of teachers leave the profession within five years of joining it.

In the end, the responsibility for this poor situation cannot, and does not, sit with individual schools. It is the framework – the patchwork of ill-fitting systems and regulation – in which they exist, and with which they are compelled to comply, that needs a radical rethink.

We desperately need a new era of inclusive education, ending the culture of exclusion from our schools, and supporting every child to succeed. That means extending special educational needs support, developing a greater focus on nurture and therapeutic support for vulnerable children, and challenging Ofsted (the Office for Standards in Education, Children's Services and Skills) to live up to its strap line: 'raising standards, improving lives'.

However, whichever way you look at it, it is central government that is responsible for the policies, funding, level of regulation or freedom and innovation around education. Therefore, it is they who must be held accountable for where any child ends up in life.

This brings us on to the bigger picture. Delivering a high-quality inclusive education to children and young people is a good start, but it will never be enough.

Let's do the maths. Our state schools open for 190 days a year, most offering a school day of between six and seven hours. So that's 175 days when they are not in school at all. And, even with attendance at every after-school club and holiday activity possible, this still amounts to well under 20% of a child's overall time. The vast majority is spent elsewhere. So, where are they? What are they experiencing? And, what are they learning?

If schools provide 'formal education', youth clubs have traditionally been their hardworking cousin; wrapping vital support and 'informal education' around young people out of school hours. But since 2010, as a result of the constantly mounting financial pressure on local authorities, coupled with the depleted reserves of youth charities, the decline of the youth service has been brutal. The way I see it, this is nothing short of a societal catastrophe which has robbed countless teens of safe spaces where they can enjoy being young and the sense of belonging.

My own story – my sense of vision and purpose – was birthed and supported by a youth club, rather than a school. My youth workers knew me, they invested in me, advised and supported me. It was one of them who taught me to play the guitar, who gave me my first opportunities for leadership and public speaking, and who then helped me set up and run a youth club myself. It is literally true that I have no idea where I would be now without the safe harbour, care and time they gave me.

A typical adolescent who has benefited from a stable and secure attachment with their primary caregivers and is developmentally healthy, is still far more likely than an adult to act on impulse, to misread or misinterpret social cues and emotions, to be anxious about their image and whether people like them, to get into accidents of all kinds, and to engage in dangerous and risky behaviour. They're also less likely to think before they act, less likely to pause to consider the consequences of their actions and less likely to reconsider those reckless behaviours.

All this used to be put down to raging hormones. Until very recently, the assumption was that all the important brain development happened in the first few years of childhood. But over the last twenty years, longitudinal MRI brain scanning studies that began with children who have now reached adulthood tell us a completely different story.

Although we've talked much about neurodevelopment in terms of the early years of childhood, in recent years we've discovered that the brain is also changing fast throughout adolescence – the years between puberty and full adulthood. The transition of a new-born baby into eventual adulthood, both physically and mentally, is a gradual and intangible process.

Adolescence is a distinct stage of brain development. The brain of a typical adolescent is different from that of a child, but also from that of an adult. The brain is plastic and keeps developing throughout childhood and then across the various stages of adolescence into adulthood. This brings us back to the prefrontal cortex. We now know that, whereas development in other parts of the brain is beginning to slow down during adolescence, the prefrontal cortex – the very area of the brain responsible for decision-making, judgement, risk-taking, social interaction, social understanding, self-awareness, self-analysis and reflection – continues to develop and does not mature until well into young adulthood. Instead, an adolescent's decision-making, problem-solving and behaviour all tend to be guided more by the emotional and reactive part of the brain, called the amygdala, than by the thoughtful and logical prefrontal cortex. This makes them self-conscious, sensitive and prone to becoming extremely embarrassed about what others think of them, and often reckless.

That's why questions like 'Who am I?' and 'Where do I fit in?' become so important during teenage years. Throughout adolescence, a young person is literally in the process of inventing their identity. Of course, not every adolescent's development is identical but, that said, it's in our teens that these traits will peak. And the less secure and uncertain their childhood has been, and the more complex trauma they have endured, the more challenging and uncertain the journey into adulthood will be.

It's in the light of these facts that the long-term consequences of the neglect of organised youth work are hard to underestimate. Good youth work creates a protective layer for all young people within its sphere. Youth workers offer young people safe spaces within which to explore their identity, increase their confidence, develop their inter-personal skills, practise decision-making and think through the consequences of their actions. Youth workers offer young people safe relationships, often providing the secure attachment they have never had a chance to enjoy, or supplementing those that have guided them in earlier years, by creating a space to test whether they are seen and heard, and proving they are loved rather than unlovable.

The decline of this vital support through lack of consistent funding for youth work, both statutory and even more importantly voluntary, cannot be disassociated from the rising tide of knife and gun crime, the mental health crisis and the sense of isolation that is impacting so many young people.

The reinvention of an effective youth service, working alongside and in tandem with our schools, in a relationship of mutual respect, is a critical piece of social infrastructure we can no longer afford to ignore. To put it bluntly: without youth work, education is bust!

Before I launched Oasis I was a local youth worker – perhaps a better term would be a youth professional – in Kent. I spent much of my time in and out of all the secondary schools in the town. But it never ever occurred to me that any of the teachers I knew understood anything about young people. They were experts in English language, maths or geography – not in understanding teenagers. They, in turn, never asked me about the lives of those children, their brothers and sisters, their parents, or grandparents, or the work we did with them in the evenings, at weekends or in the holidays. How weird and dysfunctional was that?

This is why, among the local communities we work in, Oasis' goal is always to bring together the various dimensions of our work – our schools and our youth, children's and family work – as a whole. To care for the development of a child in the context of their whole life, their whole family and their whole community.

When I first got to know PJ, my biggest hope for him was that he would still be alive at the age of eighteen. He had two older brothers: one was in prison and the other was a notorious local drug dealer. He also suffered from a deep and debilitating sense of anxiety and therefore a need to please and belong. He was fodder for the local gangs in the area where he lived. But today PJ is a student at a top Russell Group university. Why? In his own estimation, it is simply this: the wrap-around, personalised care that he received as a student at Oasis.

Children's education cannot be separated from their home life, from the quality of their housing, from their own health and nutrition, from their parents' health and employability, and so on. We therefore work as hard as we can to ensure that whenever and wherever possible the schools Oasis is responsible for are not just 'co-located' with other community activities such as youth and family work, health programmes and community projects and so on, but that they actually work together toward the same outcomes with a joint structure.

There can be no denying that separate, 'siloed', non-integrated 'solutions' often fail to achieve the meaningful and lasting transformation they seek, simply because they overlook the interconnected and multifaceted nature of human needs. However, we might be able to support a young person in school, deliver youth work at evenings and weekends, support their wider family through our debt advice centre and their siblings as part of our employability programmes. This joined-up approach, focused around an individual and whole family, has profound and long-lasting impact. That's our magic. That's our yeast!

Vulnerable and isolated families become even more vulnerable and isolated as they find themselves shunted from agency to agency and required to attend various clinics for multiple and interlinked problems in their lives, with unconnected organisations staffed by 'officers' they don't know and therefore don't trust. Already facing a range of issues, they now also find themselves navigating a complex and confusing array of service systems and networks. And the delivery model which then sits people opposite each other, across counters, desks or tables in sterile and soulless offices or rooms, simply amplifies the problem. Everything about these methods shouts, 'You're a case', rather than, 'You're a family that we respect and are here to support'. Basing services in a building doesn't work. Many families will never be relaxed enough to talk in an impersonal office setting. The whole process robs them of agency, and creates trauma, rather than empowering them.

We have tolerated a system for too long that puts so much emphasis on box ticking, and is so reluctant to take a chance on doing things differently. How have we ended up with so many multi-agency meetings about every vulnerable child, which last longer than the amount of time any of the professionals in the room for that discussion will have ever spent with the child concerned? Why are we surrounding some vulnerable children with ten, and sometimes more, different professionals from different agencies, where none of them actually take the lead or build a trusted relationship with the child or family concerned? Why do our systems do so much to stifle relationship building and hold back innovation, and why are they so risk averse? In contrast to this approach, we have learned that a broad range of integrated services delivered in a relational and community-led manner has impact beyond that of any of its individual elements. The ability to be able to connect advice and support work with our educational offer, or to integrate youth work with health and wellbeing programmes, means that it is possible to support individuals in a holistic and yet personal manner.

The needs of children and their families cannot be addressed in individual silos that are not connected: educational, social, emotional, economic, spiritual and physical. That's why we need an integrated system, rather than the disjointed, ineffective and over-expensive muddle we have at the moment. Work that is not holistic will always be suboptimal, simply because it dismembers an individual's interdependent needs.

And this is the problem with 'service delivery'. Service delivery has a very narrow lens. It puts money into specific initiatives and quick 'results'. It's blinkered to the wider needs of the community, simply because it is not employed to notice them. But, because of this, it tends to deal with the symptoms: addictions, health and weight issues and so on, rather than exploring the causes of these poverties. It focuses on the presenting need of the day – what it is being paid for – rather than making the necessary investments to reduce tomorrow's risk. Then, when the money runs out, it's gone too!

Genuine community development requires a longer-term approach, one with a wider lens, because the currency for long-term systemic change is trust, and trust comes through taking time to form healthy relationships, rather than frantically running a programme in order to get the right ticks in the right boxes. That's the difference between service delivery projects and authentic community development.

Funding pots will come, and funding pots will go, but a good community development worker knows that it's people not programmes that bring change. That's why being there for the long haul, whether flushed with funding or not, is critical and it's why building trust through developing relationships is the mainstay of all community development work.

Back in September 2003, I came to work in Waterloo as a volunteer in my spare time. I became the leader of what was called Christchurch and Upton Chapel, a church with a very small congregation but a very large, empty, dilapidated building. The needs of the community were huge, but the members of the church had little or no contact with them, and we had no money.

One weekend, a young girl named Harriet, who lived on the housing estate next to the church building, died of a sudden brain haemorrhage. The tragedy for her family and the immediate community was huge. I visited her mum. I introduced myself and we chatted. She invited me in for a cup of tea. After the funeral, I suggested I pop around for another conversation. When I arrived she was there with various other members of the family, all still grieving deeply. They all told me stories of Harriet, of the joy she brought to them. So, I suggested, rather tentatively, that we might plan a celebration of her life together and invite her primary school and secondary school as well as the wider community. So, over the next six weeks or so, we worked together to put on an event for the whole community in our church building.

It proved to be a turning point. It pulled the community together. Soon we had started a regular 'stay and play' event for some of the parents we met and their toddlers; then a regular afternoon coffee and cake drop in. Twenty years on, Oasis has increasingly become the community convenor for the area, collaborating with many others from the statutory, not-for-profit, faith and private sectors. We've also become a real focal point for community activism, working with a large number of local volunteers on an array of projects.

In this, genuine partnership with other organisations and individuals is key. None of us have the complete answer. In order to get the job done we have to partner together; only this can create and sustain the high quality, integrated approach to health, mental health, personal and community care and development which we believe must be the vital ingredients of an effective child-first welfare system fit for the twenty-first century.

Effective community development work requires leaders of the different agencies to be relentlessly committed to working together, to be willing to be held accountable to one another and, crucially in my experience, to be working to one agreed vision and single framework of common purpose. 'Highly aligned, even though loosely coupled' is the only way forward. When this is not the case, money and time are wasted, and lives are ruined. Take the worrying story of Michael as an example of this.

The staff of Michael's school began to suspect that he was being abused at home. One day he arrived with significant bruising. As was their legal duty, they immediately referred him to social services. Because of the nature of the case, the police interviewed Michael, as was their legal duty, and consequently removed Michael from his home. He was taken into care overnight. However, when social services reviewed his case, as was their legal duty, it became clear that he did not meet their official threshold to be taken into care. Michael was therefore returned home the next day. This made his domestic situation worse than ever and at the same time eroded his trust in his school, also destroying his confidence in both the police and social services. Everyone in the system was doing their job and following the rules, but as a result a child was sent back into the family where, with relationships broken, his situation became more dangerous than ever.

Michael continued to get knocked around by his father, but knew very well that if he went to school, the bruises inflicted on him would be seen by his teachers, and that his school would have to take action, as was their legal duty. He knew that this would result in both police and social services becoming involved again, and things would get even worse. So, instead Michael chose regularly to be out of school.

This made him vulnerable to his local gang. Hanging around on his estate, he was gently groomed by them: picked up, talked to, made to feel important, listened to, given a sense of status. He was made to feel popular – as though somebody cared. At home he was nothing, but with the gang he felt special. That's the way gang recruitment works. He was told he owed them money. That the gifts he had received from them – trainers and cash – were never free, they were investments. He began to be forced to deliver drugs onto another gang's territory. He started carrying a knife to protect himself.

Several months ago, Michael stabbed another boy while under orders to deliver drugs – he claims, in self-defence. He will go on trial soon, and is likely to receive a custodial sentence.

We *have* to get joined up.

And, this joining up has to start at government level. Instead of a Department for Education, perhaps we need a Department, or better still a 'Ministry' (which means a service), for Children, Schools, Youth and Families. Renaming something doesn't do the job – but at least it points you in the right direction.

Principle seven
Do things 'with' people, not 'to' them or 'for' them

At school, like most children, I was taught Charles Darwin's theory of evolution: the 'survival of the fittest'. However, in the last few years a growing amount of research has begun to talk instead of the 'survival of the friendliest'.

How did our ancient ancestors survive? In terms of their physical safety, neither of the options of 'fight or flight' was viable as an escape from their fiercest predators. It was impossible to outsprint a sabre-toothed tiger, and who would have ever stood a chance in a single-handed battle with one? The truth is that we humans are only still around because we learned to work together. We learned to collaborate. Cooperation rather than competition has been key to our evolutionary success.[27]

Homo sapiens have walked the planet for at least the last 200,000 years. And those large and complex brains of ours have developed over that time to be perfectly suited to life in the small and close-knit communities in which almost everyone lived for around the

---

27 Charles Darwin is known for the survival of the fittest theory of natural selection, the common understanding of which is the famous 'dog eat dog' view that the most able and aggressive animals will continue to evolve, while weaker species will be eliminated over time. However, in 2020, Duke University researchers Brian Hare and Vanessa Woods published *Survival of the Friendliest*, in which they offer a new interpretation of Darwin's famous theory, suggesting that species that partner and cooperate with others are more likely to endure. Indeed, researchers often quote Darwin himself as stating, 'In the long history of humankind (and animal kind, too) those who learned to collaborate and improvise most effectively have prevailed', and it is very clear from his later writings that this is how he came to understand the survival of the fittest. *Survival of the Friendliest: Understanding Our Origins and Rediscovering Our Common Humanity*, is published by Random House.

first 199,800 of those 200,000 years. Across the millennia we have adapted – both neurologically and biologically – to live in multi-family, multi-generational environments, where adults, children and young people mix together in close relationship to provide us with the breadth of connections we need to thrive.

Today, our challenge is that in our modern chaotic world, it has become increasingly difficult to find that same sense of deep and genuine community. Over the last couple of centuries we've chosen to experiment with a different kind of living, and it is causing countless problems. Loneliness has become one of the most universal sources of human suffering of our age. Advances in our transport systems and communications technology happen at an extraordinary pace, but the wisdom that we require to deal with the changes this brings to us, without it destroying us, is harder to find.

The irony of all this, of course, is that most of us live in closer proximity to more people than at any other point in history. We're surrounded by them. Everywhere. But somehow, we find ourselves lost in the crowd. Worse than that, as we've become gradually more isolated from one another, we've even begun to regard this self-contained separation with a certain amount of pride. Those who appear to be able to function without significant support from others are described as independent and self-reliant, while a need for a shoulder to cry on is regarded by some as evidence of weakness rather than strength. In this context, it is perhaps worth reflecting on some of our popular ideas of masculinity, alongside the fact that the UK suicide rate is three times higher for men than for women.

In the busyness and atomisation of modern life, it's too easy to either neglect to build, or have little time to build, those all-important, mutually supportive relationships upon which both our physical and mental health are so reliant. Perhaps, however, the coronavirus crisis, by forcing us to live in isolation from one another, enabled us to realise, at least for a moment, that autonomy is never liberation and that if the value our society really does prize above all others is freedom, it is high time we invested more intentionally in community.

Community makes us whole: community creates balance. We need both to know and to be known. We are social animals. At core we are relational. We crave being seen, heard, loved and treasured. We flourish when we are connected and struggle when we're not.

We text, tweet and post, but talk less and as a result our conversational skills are declining. At home, at work, at school, we spend hours and hours in front of various screens: television, video games, mobile phones and laptops. Added to which, the media constantly focuses on and sometimes overdramatises situations of doom and gloom that we cannot change, leaving us feeling detached and impotent. And because all this is relatively new, we're not far enough down the road to really understand its full impact on a child's or an adolescent's brain development.

It's not just our children though; it's all of us. We have never been 'connected' to so many, and yet actually known by so few people. We spend our time constantly checking on the lives of those we don't know and will never meet, but know little if anything about the circumstances and needs of those we regularly bump into at the bus stop or corner store. More of us live alone and fewer of us than ever sit at a table to eat with our neighbours, or even our families. However, our social media cannot satisfy our emotional needs. So as our digital literacy has grown, our rates of anxiety, depression and suicide have done so too.

This disconnection is a form of social and emotional starvation. There is a direct relationship between a person's degree of social isolation and their risk of poor physical and mental health. To be known, to be loved, to love and to belong is far better for good physical and mental health than all those over-expensive supplements and multi-vitamins put together. Remember the 'wider determinants of health' we talked about in chapter 2?

Back in those tribes and village communities that we Homo sapiens have inhabited throughout our history, children grew up within the safety of a network of trusted, intergenerational relationships. They were nurtured, disciplined and cared for by the whole community, both women and men, as they grew through infancy, childhood and adolescence into maturity. No one adult, mother or father or grandparent, was ever expected to be able to take responsibility for this journey alone. Humans were not designed to raise children in isolation. Each member of the tribe brought their unique set of skills and strengths to the emotional, social, physical and cognitive development of the child. We are meant for community; communities in which the task of nurturing a child belongs to the many not the few.

In our modern world, however, these tried and tested principles of human development have been squeezed to the margins. Countless families have become standalone units, living many hours away from parents, grandparents and other extended family members. A single mum or dad is expected to be, amongst other things, bread-winner, cook, cleaner, counsellor, coach, nurse, homework consultant – and to do it all alone, in sickness as in health. Behind every struggling child is a struggling parent.

It's overwhelming. And when money is tight and you're also trying to cope with poor housing, food poverty, long-term illness or unemployment, and there's never a day of rest, the task becomes impossible. It all feels too much, because it is too much.

So, the challenge ahead of us is how to rebuild strong, healthy and therapeutic local communities in this strange new world which we are struggling to adapt to, because the best predictor of both physical and mental health is always relational connectedness.

Those who are rich enough can, of course, afford professional therapy. However, even sessions with the greatest therapist in the world will achieve nothing without connectedness. For 99% of the last 200,000 years there were no professionally trained and accredited therapists or child and adolescent mental health services, although this is not to diminish their role in any way, or to suggest that our ancestors didn't suffer stress, anxiety and depression. However, experts tell us that the pillars of traditional therapeutic care through the ages were:

- the strength of connection to your community;
- a set of shared beliefs, values and tales, and the stories which carried these and gave meaning to life in your tribe;
- the use of natural, plant-derived medicines, prescribed under the guidance of a trusted healer.

The problem is that our modern-day approach has made three mistakes.

- It has neglected the wellbeing and healing power of connectedness.
- It has lost much of our shared values and story.
- It has over-medicalised our responses to trauma with its reliance on drugs.

Some years back, I had the privilege of spending a week living in a Navajo village in New Mexico. The Navajo tribe is the largest indigenous tribe in the United States today. The Navajo nation's land is closed to non-Navajos unless you've been granted a permit or, in my case, given an invitation. A group of Navajo leaders had asked me to spend a week with them discussing community development and spirituality. It was a week that changed my life. I have no idea what I contributed to them – but their contribution to me was enormous.

One of the things that struck me was that everyone I spoke to introduced themselves to me in terms of their family connections.

'I am Doba, daughter of Nino', or 'I am Elu, son of Mato', they would say, before spending time telling me more about their family than themselves. At the end of each day there were huge community meals, along with much laughter and storytelling about the lives and exploits of the generations that came before. For these people, the importance of connectedness was everything.

At the end of the week, there was a wedding and to my surprise I was asked to stay for it. The celebrations, they explained, would stretch over three days. I had to get back home, but managed to change my travel arrangements so that I could stay for the first day. They called it the bride's day. That morning the whole community gathered together on what, in our culture, we might call the village green – although it was more brown than green. Everyone sat around chatting, laughing and enjoying the sun. Then one of the leaders blew a horn and with that the women of the village began to gather together in the centre of the community area. First the bride with her mother and sisters, two grandmothers and one great-grandmother. Then a collection of aunts, great-aunts, sisters-in-law, cousins, nieces, and lastly all the other women in the village: old, young, girls and babies in arms.

Now the horn was sounded again, and as the whole community danced and sang, the women formed into a huge triangle, with the bride at the head and her mother behind her with her hands around her daughter's waist. Then came the two grandmothers holding their daughters in the same way. That was followed by the great-grandmother, and then the huge crowd of others. As everyone sang, and joined together arm in arm, the women began to dance their way off the green and eventually out of sight, slowly circling the whole village before returning to the spot where they began.

I asked one of the group of men I was sitting with what all this was about. He looked a little surprised. 'It's a marriage,' he said.

'So, where is the groom?' I asked.

He laughed. 'He will get his day tomorrow. Today is for his bride. How can she be the woman, the wife and mother she wants to be without the support of her mother, her grandmothers, and all the other women of this community?' he asked, before adding with a big smile, 'And tomorrow we will dance to support the groom, while the women get their turn to watch.'

Stress is always magnified in the echo chamber of your own head. But a good multi-family, multi-generational community is a healing community, one which is filled with countless informal therapeutic moments and interactions. There may be no formal therapy sessions, but there's a myriad of social connections that together build resilience, wisdom and hope. Most of the world's very best support and healing happens naturally, without professional involvement, in small communities – it always has.

And there's another important dimension to this. The way in which we all learn most in life is through our failures. Strong and caring intergenerational communities allow you to fail. They let you mess up without rejecting or shaming you. They support you. It's only in the safety of an intergenerational community where people have learned the greatest lesson, that what we invest in others is the most valuable gift we can ever give. When we are in a place of the self-understanding that sets us free to do so, we can find the support we need to grow. The following episode is a perfect example of intergenerational support.

Timothy was eight, and of Columbian descent. He was given a school project, to research life in London during the Second World War. Sid, a thoroughbred cockney, in his eighties, had been a printer on a national newspaper all his working life which, as a young man, included the years of the war. Both were part of our church. So I introduced them to one another. The result: Timothy's project was the best in the class, and Sid found a new energy and vitality as he had the chance to retell his stories. Both of them discovered a deep and lasting friendship: one that spanned several generations and linked two very different cultures.

A few years later, Sid died. I took his funeral. Timothy and his mum were in the congregation. As the presiding minister, I rode from the church building to the cemetery in the lead hearse with Sid's coffin. As the hearse pulled slowly away, there I saw Timothy, standing on the pavement, crying for the loss of his dear friend.

Where do you find depth of community like that? A young boy's life enriched, deepened, changed, strengthened, broadened by his friendship with an elderly man, seven decades older than him, from a very different culture. It was beautiful.

People often tell me that they'd love to come to our church, but they don't believe in God. My response is always the same. 'Whatever you do, don't let something like that get in your way.' The same is also true, of course, of all other open, welcoming and non-judgemental faith and community groups. Where else, in our society, can you find this kind of multi-cultural, intergenerational community belonging?

Poverty will never be solved by programmes. A caring society springs not from the diktats of Whitehall, but from real day-to-day contact with, and concern for, our neighbours and involvement with local community. Government can do certain things very well, but the fact is that because local community groups are on the ground and are trusted, they are able to respond faster and with more sensitivity to real needs, and to do so with a level of knowledge and care that it is impossible for statutory bodies to achieve. Because of this, they are far more effective in their work than the expensive initiatives of government will ever be.

The problem is that the state doesn't like anything that isn't formal and communities are by their very nature informal. But democracy, as Abraham Lincoln famously expressed, should be 'the government of the people by the people'. In other words, true democracy requires active community involvement. When the democratic process is monopolised by government and professionals, it is hugely weakened and our communities, indeed the whole of society, pays a very heavy price.

It's extremely short-sighted to believe that either government or statutory agencies can do the job of community development. Instead, we need that new social covenant I have already spoken of. A civil contract that ends the 'nanny state' by creating a mature partnership between government, local authorities and local neighbourhoods, which empowers ordinary people and whole communities. It has to be properly funded, but to say it again, nothing other than this model will work, however many noughts there are at the end of the budget thrown at it.

A great example of this was the civic response to Covid during the first national lockdown. No one paid the groups who spontaneously volunteered to sew and donate makeshift protective masks and scrub bags for healthcare workers. No one drew on government payments to help elderly neighbours. No government decree ordered over one million people to volunteer to help the NHS. Instead, serving others became as contagious as the virus itself.

A friend of mine lived through the horror of the Grenfell Tower fire back in 2017, which claimed the lives of seventy-two people. He has worked with the community over the years since, and put it like this, 'You just can't overestimate the significance of local faith and community groups. That's what we learned in the aftermath. The bodies that were most effective were not those of central or local government. It was the local community groups, churches, mosques, community organisations – they were on the ground, they were trusted and they were fleeter of foot.' In that context, listen to the words of Mark Carney, who served as the governor of the Bank of England from 2013 to 2020, in his Reith Lecture for the BBC in 2020:

> *When we outsource civic virtue to paid third-party providers, we narrow the scope of society and encourage people to withdraw from it. There is extensive evidence of the commercialisation effect. When people are engaged in an activity that they see as intrinsically valuable, offering them money weakens their motivation by depreciating, or even crowding out, their intrinsic interests or commitments. In these ways, the spread of the market could undermine community, one of the most important determinants of happiness.*

The move to professionalisation easily ignores, overrides and replaces the informal. I've seen it happen from time to time within Oasis. A new community project starts as an Oasis leader works with and inspires volunteers to work together to meet a local need. As a result, the project becomes successful and grows – but in that process it professionalises, and if we are not careful there is less space for the contribution of amateurs. Ironically, however, if the amateurs are squeezed out, the project begins to lose its grassroots feel and street knowledge, and what the health service likes to refer to as 'social prescribing' is also lost.

Though children and families exist in an ecosystem of relationships, statutory children's and family services often bypass these relationships and act in isolation from them. Too often their work feels like something 'done to people' rather than a healthy partnership with them. 'Nothing about us, without us', as the disability rights activist James Charlton said. This over-professionalisation of support has corroded not only community engagement and ownership, but also the very sense of community itself. Instead of deepening and strengthening local ownership and enhancing relationships, it has disempowered and robbed families of a sense of honour and dignity.

We have paralysed informal community networks by profession-alising care. We obsess over the minutiae of health and safety, safeguarding and risk assessments, but our lack of investment in building a network of informal care, combined with under-resourced professional care, has created huge risk and destroys both health and safety. So, for instance, while waiting lists for child mental health services are the longest they've ever been – and that's for the minority who are fortunate enough to make it onto the list in the first place – it's illegal to use a good friend to regularly look after a child under eight years of age for more than two hours a day unless they qualify as a registered childminder! That good friend could just offer a preventative layer around mental health issues – for a child, or indeed a parent.

It's a classic example of making a policy with good intentions, but minimal understanding of the developmental needs of children or the strength and importance of community. There are many more!

Delivering services 'to' local people or 'for' them is always disem-powering. Real and lasting transformation is only fuelled as we empower individuals and whole communities to become change makers themselves. When the people who have the power to make decisions do not look like or think like the communities that they are trying to serve, everything is set up for failure. As Darren McGarvey explains in his book *The Social Distance Between Us: How Remote Politics Wrecked Britain*, the distance, whether geo-graphical, economic or cultural, between those who make the decisions and the people who are on the receiving end of them, means that even those with the noblest aims inadvertently cause harm as a result of their social remoteness.[28]

Even when professionals consult with a community, it's often a tokenistic, box-ticking exercise rather than an authentic process

---

28 Darren McGarvey, *The Social Distance Between Us: How Remote Politics Wrecked Britain* (London: Ebury, 2022).

for listening. This simply disempowers them and leaves the community feeling unheard rather than listened to and valued. Genuine community consultation should create a tangible sense of community participation, engagement and collaboration around what's really needed, and how any service could be best provided.

To address this issue, the concept of what is known as 'kinship care' was first introduced in New Zealand back in 1989 with extraordinary results. Whenever a child has to be taken into care, kinship care seeks to give priority to the voice and wisdom of the wider family: a practice which is built on the core belief that, although most abuse takes place within a family, the same family will also be the most committed to keeping the child safe.

Kinship care represented a very significant shift in terms of where the responsibility sits for children in need of care. Rather than weakening or breaking the links and relationships of a child with their wider family, kinship care is based on the very opposite: continuity. Where are the protective relationships in the family? Children are kept within their own community and family wherever possible by inviting families to be part of the decision-making process about the future of their 'kin' or children. Of course, there are a whole number of formal aspects to the assessment process: social work interviews, police, referee checks, a medical assessment of the carers and of their home and so on, but these are carried out sensitively, relationally and with form filling kept to an absolute minimum.

Although the wider extended family often want to step up and be involved, due to their own financial circumstances they are just as often unable to help. To compensate for this, as the system has developed, it's also been recognised that there is a need for careful support for family members – often grandparents – as they adjust to their new roles as caregivers in terms of the financial, social, and mental-health challenges they find themselves taking on.

Over the years, this way of building support around the care arrangements for a child has not only proved extremely beneficial both to the children involved and to those who take on the caring, but it is also much more efficient in terms of expense for local authority budgets. What's more, as each family's perspectives and critiques of the system are heard, the system is improved and becomes more effective: the whole thing becomes a virtuous circle.

The principle that working to keep children within their family and cultural context is the best way of caring for those who have suffered abuse or neglect, both in the short- and in the longer-term, has now been adopted and adapted to fit the cultural needs of a growing number of countries. As part of this, kinship care is now playing an increasingly important role in the UK, where currently it's estimated that there are some 150,000 kinship carers. Around half of kinship carers are grandparents, although other relatives including older siblings, aunts and uncles, as well as family friends and neighbours, also serve in this way.

The vast majority of these arrangements are still informal – community doing what community does – a child comes to live with extended family members either full-time or for most of the time because their parents aren't able to care for them. However, increasingly, what are known as 'special guardianship' or 'child arrangements' orders are made by a family court. All this represents a welcome breakthrough, but there is still no national mechanism to support kinship carers in their commitment, which by its very nature can stretch resources and create both domestic and financial pressures.

Financial, legal and therapeutic support are all essential, as is training, and the extension of the same rights and recognition to kinship carers as are given to adoptive parents. None of this exists at the moment. And, although it is encouraging that, at the beginning of 2023, as part of their response to the 2022 independent review of children's social care, government announced its intention to begin to explore the creation of the first ever national strategy around kinship care, its development is urgent!

Right now, I listen to wider family members who all too often feel ignored, treated as 'a case' rather than 'a family', disempowered and pre-judged by professional practitioners, often including our child protection system. We need a mindset change. We need our systems – all our systems – and the practitioners involved with any particular family, to work much harder to develop practices which build far stronger foundations to establish trust, which shift power away from those who deliver services and share it within the community, giving as many who will the opportunity of contributing and finding their voice.

But it's not just our existing child welfare; our educational, mental health and juvenile justice systems all have the tendency to do the same thing. Too many of their policies and practices marginalise, shame and fragment families and undermine community.

Our current over-reliance on professionals is not only a therapeutic and relational disaster, it's also a resource disaster. The two issues play right into one another. Not only does it ignore the strengths and bypass the informal networks in the community, negating its insights and wasting its talent, but worse, it runs the huge risk of angering and alienating those it was designed to help. Partnership enhances community robustness: an over reliance on professionalism destroys it.

Jack, a twelve-year-old boy with a difficult family background and prone to sudden, sometimes violent mood swings, was a student at an Oasis school. I really struggled to engage with Jack. In fact, try as I might, I couldn't even get him to make eye contact. Then, one Thursday morning, a man in his mid-80s arrived at the unit where we provided education for Jack. I was visiting as well. And so it was that Philip introduced himself to me and enthusiastically explained he'd 'popped in' to spend some time with Jack, which he did a couple of times each week.

The anti-social Jack sauntered over to meet him. Philip smiled. Jack smiled back. I was intrigued. Philip made Jack a mug of tea before they wandered casually across to the pool table. Jack handed Philip a cue. But, as the game progressed, it became clear that Philip was going to win, easily!

The problem was that Jack was not good with defeat. He found it humiliating and was quite capable of switching suddenly and lashing out.

Philip hit the black perfectly and it gently rolled into a corner pocket. I waited for Jack's reaction. But instead of flying into a temper, he smiled. 'Well done,' he muttered.

'You're getting good at this,' responded Philip. 'It won't be long before I'm congratulating you.' They wandered back to the kitchen and – with more tea in hand – headed for a computer to work on a 'catch-up' literacy programme together. It was then that the penny dropped. The reason Philip's relationship with Jack was so powerful was that Philip was a volunteer.

I suddenly realised that the only adults who normally gave Jack any attention were professionals – like me – those who were paid to be with him: teachers, social workers, youth workers and counsellors. But Philip was different. He was there simply because he chose to be. No one was paying him and that's what had such a huge impact on Jack. Someone had chosen to invest in him, just for the sake of it: it was transformational!

The volunteer, or to use their other name the 'amateur' – which as all French speakers know comes from the word meaning 'lover of' – has an essential role to play in any effective integrated health service of the future. Our society desperately needs to grow many more amateurs!

Whereas statutory services often claim that grassroots organisations and individuals are hard to work with, perhaps, in truth, things are the other way around. The professional language, the abbreviations and ever-changing acronyms, are for most frightening and extremely excluding. Put differently, they serve to achieve the very opposite of the goals and targets that so many of them were originally articulated to help us reach.

More than that, because children and young people in particular look for security through continuity with those who work with them, professional short-termism is a serious problem. Relationships are frequently exited too early and long before the originally agreed outcomes are achieved. This simply retraumatises those who already believe that they are not enough. Relational continuity is essential to good long-term outcomes.

We must learn to work with the power of community, instead of inadvertently ignoring, overriding or replacing it; to spot the existing informal, as well as formal, networks, skills and strengths in a community, and to partner with them – turning recipients into providers. And that means actively engaging community members and grassroots groups in designing, delivering and leading services.

Social services only have the scope to work with children who are seriously at risk, either at home or outside of the home, or who are suffering significant harm. That means aside from having a huge and positive impact, these informal community relationships – sometimes referred to as 'low-level' therapeutic care – also help stop professional systems becoming clogged up and overloaded with referrals that they don't have the capacity to meet.

The sacred responsibility of nurturing and protecting children, young people and families cannot be left to a few specialist agencies. Rather, this is the job of the whole community. If we want to keep children safe from harm, as well as ensure that parents and carers enjoy the resources they need to love and support them, the way we 'do' community must be revisited.

'It takes a village to raise a child' is one of the most over-quoted phrases of the last decade. But our problem is that, although we sign up to the doctrine, at the very same time we have failed to invest in building or supporting that philosophy, and instead have simply left things to a bunch of paid professionals.

Until we all understand this and are prepared to do something about it, we are lost!

Principle eight
Trust is the glue of life

The story is told of a government representative who paid a visit to a small farm. The farm was owned and run by a married couple who were enjoying a short break over a cup of coffee, while also keeping a close eye on their eight-year-old daughter who was playing in the farmyard. The government visitor asked the girl if her mum and dad were around, but as he was doing this, the girl's mother happened to look out of the open kitchen window to see her young daughter talking to a stranger. Horrified, she called out at the top of her voice, 'Who are you talking to? Get in here, right now!'

'It's OK, Mummy,' came the unconcerned response. 'He says he's from the government.'

'Well, in that case, get in here and bring the cow with you!'

Trust is a little word, the presence or absence of which has huge ramifications. Trust is integral to any successful relationship, organisation or partnership. And distrust – the outcome of the breakdown of trust – is extremely expensive at every level of society. When trust goes missing we are doomed to dysfunction: we grow frustrated, we withdraw, we cease to engage and relationships fail. And where relationships fail, everything fails.

Society is nothing if not a complex web of relationships held in place by trust, built around promises made and promises kept, and trust in government and its statutory services is an essential foundation of social cohesion. But in recent years continued revelations of mismanagement, bad behaviour, poor governance, scandals and coverups in Whitehall, and the town hall, have soured that trust.

Distrust of central and local government, as well as of police, big business, the Church and of authority in general, has become deeply embedded in our society. So, the big question is, in a society where trust has been so badly eroded, how can it be restored? And how do we rebuild it?

Trust is like money in the bank. Though one withdrawal will not necessarily take you into the red, if over time funds only ever flow out, eventually even the richest account will be emptied. However, the reverse is also true: the more deposits you make, however small, the more credit you collect.

The build-up or breakdown of trust is normally incremental. Even though, in some cases, a single act of betrayal is enough to destroy trust immediately, most of the time it ebbs and flows. Therefore, the fact that trust has become such a scarce commodity in our society of late can only mean that we perceive ourselves to have been disappointed very often.

One symptom of this lack of trust is the way that so many people choose to avoid statutory services whenever they possibly can. 'Don't you dare tell a social worker about us. The last thing we need is them interfering,' is, for instance, a sentiment I hear expressed too often.

Rather than feeling empowered or supported, we feel that the authorities are spying on us, reporting on us, judging us and, worse than that, judging us by their own distorted criteria. And at the same time, lacking any sense of accountability to us – the payers of tax and council tax – they appear aloof and officious, while also undervaluing, or even completely disregarding, our efforts to contribute.

This breakdown of trust has been hugely exacerbated by the move to the so called 'efficiency' of online communication. For example, it's frustrating to find yourself lost in an unintuitive website that refuses to give you the choices or information you need, and then freezes you out; or to be asked by a robot voice to wait in a long phone queue, listening to piped music, only to be told eventually that the service is shut, and that you should dial another number or call again tomorrow. Complicating things even further, countless people can't use a digital device, which means our new 'efficiency' can't reach a lot of the most at-need people at all. It turns out that being efficient is not the same thing as being effective and sometimes is the exact opposite. Ironically, therefore, in losing their human dimension, these 'support' services also lose the very efficiency they were seeking to create in the first place!

But there's a double irony in this. Often it turns out to be the poorly and inconsistently funded local charities – staffed by volunteers with local knowledge and lived experience of trying to access these very same services – that end up stepping in to offer the advice and advocacy to those who have lost trust in the very expensive statutory systems that supposedly exist to support them.

I've already told you the story of how, back in the mid-1980s, my wife and I set up a safe house, to provide accommodation for young people who had been rejected or exploited by those who should have loved and cared for them.

Well, the bit I didn't explain is that before we opened or even had a house, I booked an appointment with the head of housing for the local authority we wanted to work in. At the age of twenty-nine, I went to see him, filled with excitement and no doubt huge amounts of naivety. Having told him what we wanted to do and asked for his help, he looked at me, paused and then said, 'I don't like you.' He clearly wasn't a man to mince his words. 'We don't need any hostels run by your type around here,' he added. 'Leave it to the professionals. If you open, it'll be over my dead body!' Well, I don't know what happened to him, but we did open.

It took four years to turn our vision into a reality, but we got there. Our approach worked – and it still does. In fact, that same local council now has a very different view of us. Not only have we become their trusted partner, but in spite of the vehement pro-tests of that head of housing back in the 1980s, they've now given us oversight of all supported housing for young adults across the borough.

Whether it's between government and communities, or local authorities and community organisations, trust is never a simple 'on or off' affair. It's a living entity. It develops slowly. There's simply no shortcut. Trust is built over time.

One of the core issues when it comes to partnership between gov-ernment and communities is funding. When government looks to the voluntary sector for partnership, what it hopes for is a very steady camel. A camel can go for days without any water, and for weeks without food. It comes with its own nutritional supplies courtesy of a hump or two. More than that, a camel can carry a heavy load and yet still walk many miles each day through the harshest desert climate: burning heat by day and freezing cold by night. What's more, a camel's unusual gait and wide feet allow it to move quickly through the toughest terrain without sinking into the sand. The problem, from the government's point of view, is that what it often gets when it attempts to partner with the voluntary sector feels more like an unruly group of wild and spiteful cats, who refuse to work together and fight over any available food. The collective noun for wild cats is very appropriately a 'destruction'!

But there are two sides to this story. Charities are often compelled to compete with each other, rather than to cooperate, because of the short-sightedness of both national and local government funding systems. These often lack any sense of clear vision, are overly bureaucratic, administered by people who don't understand the nature of the communities they are making decisions about and offer nothing more than short-term funding focused on superficial outcomes. On top of this, the big national charities, with full-time professional fundraising and bid-writing teams, regularly outbid small local charities, even though their understanding of and commitment to the communities and issues the funding is trying to address are nowhere near those of the grassroots movements.

Small but effective local grassroots charities that are already doing the job on a shoestring end up working crazy hours to answer stupid questions in order to meet unrealistic funding bid deadlines, only to be informed by impersonal emails that their applications have not been successful. And then, once the funding is gone, and those who won it are gone with it, that same little charity – if it's managed to survive – is once again left to pick up the pieces. So it is that the depressing cycle begins again. It's all a ridiculous waste of time, money, passion, talent and expertise, as well as the cause of huge frustration, local anger and the erosion of trust. The real issue is, of course, not simply funding but even more than that, the continuity of delivery.

Next month, the funding for a project that we've run for the last four years for a government agency around health and nutrition in a local community in which we are based comes to an end. Everyone agrees the outcomes we've achieved have been great, but in spite of that, the national programme from which our funding comes is being closed. We have already been invited to reapply for the new funding opportunity which opens in eight weeks' time. The problem, however, is that although we can bid, and indeed may well be successful, we won't know the outcome until the end of next summer. We don't have any bridging money, so we will have to make staff redundant and we will lose their skills and the relationships they have built in the community. Then we will have to recruit, train and mobilise new staff.

This has been part of Oasis' story over the years. Though we are a national charity, because the focus of our work is in small communities across the country, employing and empowering local staff, this same problem still hits us and still hurts us.

A few years ago we had the opportunity of working with a particular large NHS trust. Their key officers had been to see our work elsewhere and loved it. Out of this came the idea that we might work alongside them in one of the most socially and economically deprived communities within their patch. They had been struggling with the scale and cost of chronic health needs there for many years. We had several planning meetings around this with them. The idea was that Oasis would embed a community development practitioner to work alongside the GPs and also build bridges with others in the community – the primary school, the nursery, the community centre, the pub, the church, and most importantly local people – in order to get them all working together. What the NHS call 'social prescribing'.

But when it came to funding us, we were told that money could only be made available to us for twelve months with no guarantee for the next year. We had put in a five-year budget. Three lines of questioning followed from the bosses. Why was the salary bill so high? It really wasn't – it was less than half of what anyone questioning us was paid. Why didn't we appoint a less experienced person to fill this role? Our answer was, of course, that community development or organising work requires real skill, experience and expertise. Why did we need a commitment to more than twelve months? Because twelve months is impossible, we said. A good community worker will take most of that first year to build relationships with local people, discover their strengths, listen to their understanding of community needs and empower them to lead. All of which is worse than pointless if you won't commit to the long term. And, we added, what about the workers themselves? How do you expect to recruit the right candidate, ask them to leave their current job, move their whole life into a new community, and spend the first six months building relationships, only to spend the second six worried about finding another job in case the funding isn't renewed?

I've spent half my life trying to jump through hoops for funders: governmental, corporate and philanthropic. This not only wastes time, resources and emotional energy, but leaves hundreds of organisations like ours with all kinds of budgetary, employment, redundancy, recruitment, training and delivery challenges, while doing nothing to make us feel valued for our work.

If we are to build the healthy communities we know we need, all this has to change. We have to end the 'begging bowl' culture where suited and booted 'experts' control the money and are constantly spending too much of it on ideas in order to 'test' and 'measure' them, rather than trust practitioners with decades of experience. We have to relearn the essential art of working together, more closely and more intelligently, as we honour what each party has to bring to the conversation. We have no option.

In a survey some years ago, pairs of people in relationships of various types (students and teachers, husbands and wives, bosses and employees, and so on) were individually asked which of them acted in the most trustworthy way. Perhaps unsurprisingly everyone interviewed stated that they believed themselves to be the most trustworthy party in the relationship. More interestingly, however, they also universally felt that the other person in the relationship, if asked, would have to agree with their assessment. Of course, none of them did!

The first step towards becoming more trustworthy, then, is accepting that probably none of us are trusted as we believe we are or would like to be. Trust has to be worked at, not just individually, but in terms of relationships between local government and community groups as well as between those groups themselves. It's hard work for all sides, all of the time. And it's a continuing task. We all long to be trusted. But the level of trust we command is dependent on something subtly different: trustworthiness. Because the key question for us all is not so much why people don't trust us but what we can do, whether government or community group, to become worthy of trust.

The advantages of being trustworthy are very clear. The more that people trust us, the more they respect us. The more they respect us, the more they will actively seek our advice, be inclined to accept and act on our recommendations, choose to partner with us, warn us of dangers that we might avoid and feel comfortable in their relationship with us.

Over the years I've developed an equation; a set of principles that I've learned apply to the development and the maintenance of trust in all types of relationships:

$$\frac{T = C + D + R}{S}$$

Trust = Credibility + Dependability + Relationship ÷ Self-interest

Trustworthiness is created by credibility, and credibility is about our competency, capacity, skill, knowledge and resource. Those with whom we work must know that we know what we are talking about and have the expertise to deliver tangible results.

Credibility has huge implications for the level of trust we invest into any relationship. If, for example, you can't drive and a friend offers to take you out for some lessons, you will only be able to trust them if they themselves are a qualified and competent driver. We only trust people if we perceive that they have the appropriate knowledge, expertise and ability.

Dependability is all about whether or not people perceive us as being reliable and consistent.

It is about keeping promises and commitments and developing reputation. And because other people's judgements on our dependability are slowly built up over time, the more interactions we have with someone, the clearer an idea they will have about how dependable they regard us as being. In the end, dependability is a matter of track record.

We all know how amazingly easy it is to let people down. 'I'll call you later in the week', 'I'll be there at 7:30', 'You'll have an answer by Tuesday', then we find that the pressures and busyness of life get in our way. If you promise to phone someone at a certain time, you're only dependable if you do, in fact, call them at that time – or, without making a habit of it, text them to apologise and to set another date and time with them. These may seem to be small things, but it is exactly these small things that determine whether or not others regard us as being dependable. It's the length of time it takes us to reply to a voice message or an email; it's our punctuality when it comes to ringing back, making meetings, answering letters, or passing on contacts, on which we are measured for the big things. It's about delivering on what we promise to do, when we say we'll do it.

The most vital factor in building trust is relationship and ironically it is probably also the most overlooked factor. Relationship is essential to trust. What parent, for instance, would ever consider leaving their young child with a babysitter they didn't know?

Building trustworthiness is about an emotional as well as rational journey. They say, 'It's not what you know: it's who you know', but the truth is that it has to be a bit of both. Trust grows where credibility, dependability and healthy relationships are present. Working relationships are no different from the relationships we build in our personal lives. They need understanding, thoughtfulness, consideration, sensitivity, forgiveness and support, along with that rarest and most expensive form of generosity, the gift of our time. When we overlook these qualities; when we end up simply focused on getting the job done, the job never gets done.

If we invest time and energy into the people with whom we interact, it is highly likely that, just as in our home lives, things will slowly begin to run more smoothly, disagreements will be less frequent, accomplishing tasks will become more enjoyable and trust will flourish. But more than this, and again just as in private life, integrity calls us to ensure that building and deepening relationships is not just a means to an end, but rather an end in itself. When it's not, our lack of integrity – of authenticity – will soon be spotted.

Healthy relationships always require a level of vulnerability, openness and transparency, especially as they first start to develop. Though there is a risk of rejection involved in taking the first step in building a strong relationship, the only way to ensure that any relationship has a chance of growing is to initiate the relationship development yourself. Building trust always involves taking risks. In order to develop strong relationships, we must take the risk of trusting other people. If we want our relationships to grow we have to give. We have to give a favour to earn a favour. There's no other way. By giving to a relationship as much as or more than we take from it, we slowly prove ourselves to be trustworthy. And when we do make mistakes, in strong relationships we will find that we are much more easily forgiven.

However, if trust is built through a combination of credibility, dependability and relationship, it is always damaged by self-interest. It's about your levels of empathy. Do I believe you care about me and my success as well as yours? The simple truth is that however hard you try to build trust, if you give the impression that you are in it all for yourself, your efforts will be in vain.

Of course, everyone has a degree of self-interest – that's understood and accepted. So, the real question is about the level of care you have for others rather than just for yourself. How much will we genuinely work for the 'win' of our partner or employee? Dealing with anyone who is fundamentally as interested in your agenda as they are their own is an amazing experience. As Harry Truman once said, 'There is no end to what you can achieve in life, so long as you don't care who gets the credit.'

When we deliver on the small things, whether we are a government, business or charity, slowly we will find that we are trusted with bigger things: it's a law of the universe.

Although Oasis employs many staff, our goal is always to ensure that a number of key community staff are part of any neighbourhood in which we work. The 'come and go' of professionals in smart cars and smart clothes is not only dizzying to local communities, but on its own it just cannot build real trust or true partnership. You can only lead from within. It may sound obvious but the people we really trust are those we know and who, in turn, know and care about us. However, this principle is one almost universally ignored or neglected by those who fund and deliver community services.

So it is that although Oasis works in communities across the UK, in all but one of them I am – like it or not – a 'professional', albeit I hope a friendly one, who arrives in a car or on a train to 'do a job', before heading home. Only in one community, the one where I live, am I truly known.

One of the consequences of this is that the old chestnut of work/life balance is metamorphosed, because you end up 'doing life' alongside people whom other professionals would see as clients. Instead, these people are now your friends. You share the same concerns about life in the local community; you come to understand and feel the nuance, the pain, and you share the struggles and joys. You have empathy rather than simply a data set.

By its very nature government, both national and local, is blind to the specific needs, fears, hopes and concerns of a local neighbourhood. It lacks 'street knowledge'. Too often, the policies it seeks to implement have been worked out in a lecture room, on a laptop, or in a committee room, before being ratified in a boardroom – all far removed from the reality of a coalface operation. But these 'quick-fix' solutions, imposed from outside, are almost guaranteed to create more harm and hurt than good. And, even when as part of this strategising the users are consulted, this too easily becomes a paper exercise. Though it has the effect of making the decision-makers feel better, it leaves those who were 'consulted' frustrated and feeling unheard rather than understood.

The only way of overcoming this Achilles heel is for government and local councils to forge new and deeper partnerships with the voluntary sector and especially with grassroots communities, deliberately moving away from the failed master–servant attitudes of the past.

Any real, healthy community where relationships flourish necessarily exists in a small geographical area: a neighbourhood, a housing estate, a town, a village or a parish. That's why national government agencies and local authority statutory services, which cover large areas, struggle to understand them and therefore to get things done well in them. Grassroots voluntary organisations have strengths that no bureaucracy can ever match, because they're responsive, locally accountable, small and flexible enough to respond to individuals with individual attention, and to put real needs before the rules of the system.

Each and every community is different. Government and the civil service often remind me of the type of musician who has learned a couple of tunes by rote and is fine as long as they can stick to playing exactly that same tune. But, as I mentioned earlier, community development work is about learning to play jazz. The wonderful thing about a jazz musician is that they understand the structures, principles and roots behind the tune – not just the notes – so also have the ability to improvise, play with others, change key, to read the audience and adapt to the vibe of the moment. Voluntary agencies that are firmly rooted in the specific geographical communities of which they are a permanent part – 365 days a year, year in, year out – create jazz! They can bring imaginative and tailormade approaches to local issues. And that's what government just can't do.

There is, of course, an indispensable role for 'top-down' central structures, principles and coordination. But this must be held in balance with the insights of 'bottom-up' movements, which bring those principles and policies to life as they interpret them for specific local settings. This means that government, both central and local, needs to learn to think of itself as more of a support and resource base than a control room.

In the first few months of the invasion of Ukraine by Russia, as the Donbas region came under attack, the students from Oasis schools came up with an ingenious plan to raise money to support families who were becoming refugees or being made homeless in Ukraine. They wanted to support the people of the Donbas and so, together with the money they raised, they bought a 4x4 vehicle and donated it to a group of local churches to be used to deliver vital food and medical supplies very near to the frontline.

Why the local churches? Because, our students said, they were rooted in the communities. Because they were those communities. The churches were not just there to work with the dispossessed. They were the dispossessed. None of them had to do reconnaissance work to discover where the needs were. They knew the need only too well. They knew the families – many of them individually. They didn't need a GPS to navigate the area. They knew the city, the towns, the villages, the roadways, the safe routes and the short cuts. They had the local intelligence!

And alongside this key principle is another which is equally important: longevity. It takes time – far more time than a parliamentary cycle – for relationships to deepen, perspective to settle, and sustainable work to take root and develop.

One of the problems is that because national and local government works on such a short political cycle, inevitably its goals become equally short term. It is all about banner headlines, quick fixes and showy results. But long-term challenges require long-term commitments and resources, rather than the chop-and-change created by the latest political fads and soundbites: 'Big Society', 'The New Deal', 'Levelling Up', 'Tough on Crime, Tough on the Causes of Crime', 'The Many not the Few', 'Take Back Control', 'Strong and Stable', 'Back to Basics'… And the funding pots that go with them come and go – just like the politicians who promote them.

Through the chapters of this book, I've told you various stories about Oasis' work in Waterloo. The simple reason for this is the first principle I set out right at the beginning of this book: in order to understand anything about community development in general, you must first have experienced it, long-term, in micro-detail, in at least one real local community.

Waterloo is the local community where I live, where I am known, and where for the last twenty years I have worked. It was back in September 2003 that I became the leader of what was then called Christchurch and Upton Chapel. As I mentioned previously, it was a church with a very small congregation but an extremely large, empty and dilapidated building.

After several months of listening and getting to know people, I began to suggest some modest changes aimed at opening up the building and welcoming in the local community. One was as simple as moving the pulpit in the church, the current positioning of which made it impossible to use the space for any community activities. Joyce, a pensioner who had been a member of the church for many years, marched over to me one day and asked a very straightforward and pointed question, 'When are you leaving?'

I was taken aback but my answer had a directness that matched hers. 'Never,' I asserted. 'You are stuck with me. I'm going nowhere.'

Joyce's response took me by surprise. I have never forgotten it, and I learned a huge amount from it. 'Wonderful,' she said with a smile. 'In that case you can do what you like. I'm not saying I will agree with it all, but I'll support you. But remember, you've promised to stay!'

In that moment, the penny dropped. Joyce had lived through an array of 'new ministers' at the church. Each had arrived with 'their' plans and strategies. Each had taken up their role in a wave of enthusiasm and the setting out of giant promises, but within a few years each had chosen, for one reason or another, to move on. So, for Joyce, just like the rest of the congregation, what they needed to know was that I wouldn't ask them to make big changes, simply to become the latest leader to abandon them. Over time they had all grown weary of empty words and had become tired of 'strategies' they didn't own being imposed on them by people they hadn't known long enough to trust.

Principle nine
People follow people, not disembodied ideas

It was in 1960 that Chief Albert Luthuli, a Zulu South African anti-apartheid activist, became the first African-born recipient of the Nobel Peace Prize in recognition of his leadership of the non-violent struggle against racial discrimination, and his vision of a racially integrated South African society.

With his favourite cry, 'Let My People Go!' Luthuli's quiet authority became a powerful, life-shaping role model for countless younger leaders, including both Nelson Mandela and Martin Luther King Jr.[29] However, the famous inspirational phrase originates way further back in time than with Luthuli. 'Let my people go!' was Moses' demand of the Egyptian pharaoh, the despotic ruler of the land where, for 400 years, the Hebrew people had been held in slavery. But as well as this ancient, late bronze-age story is known, it still poses more than one pertinent question for our contemporary world.

Why did it take 400 years of servitude for the Hebrew people to reach this showdown moment? Had no other Hebrew, at any point over the four preceding centuries, ever succeeded in plotting a mass rebellion against Egyptian bondage and subjugation? Surely, each and every successive generation had told stories of freedom to their children, and railed against the oppression and injustice they suffered?

---

29 Luthuli even used the phrase 'Let My People Go' as the title of his autobiography.

It's impossible to believe that the Hebrew people had not written countless laments of despair and poems of hope, as they dreamed of liberty together. But somehow, in spite of all the longing, heart-ache and pain, they remained in slavery. What this enslaved nation lacked was a leader: someone with the character, courage and commitment needed to step up, galvanise and lead them into the freedom they longed for.

So, what is it that makes a visionary leader? What makes a Moses, an Albert Luthuli, a Nelson Mandela, an Emmeline Pankhurst, a Mahatma Gandhi, a Martin Luther King, a Mother Teresa, a Greta Thunberg or a Volodymyr Zelenskyy? It's an obvious truth, but it's those who follow a leader who make them one. A leader only becomes a leader when a second person chooses to work with them. But the task of people like Moses, Albert Luthuli, Martin Luther King, Mandela, Emmeline Pankhurst and the like is never simply to shout, 'Let my people go!' Much more importantly, it is to lead their people from despair to hope, from absence to abundance, from the 'old land' of servitude to a 'new land' of freedom; to articulate a narrative that creates buy-in to and shared ownership of the vision.

It's not that the visionary leader must have a detailed map of the 'promised land' to which they call us, but they do have to be able to point us in the right direction. They must have the ability to paint a picture of its benefits, to enable us to navigate the journey towards it, and they must be brave enough to move us forward, because nine times out of ten the journey also implies huge upheaval, disruption and some opposition.

I call these 'new-land' seekers 'movement' people. In order for any organisation to move forward rather than stagnate it needs at least one person who fits this description. It's essential. These are the pioneers, the blue-sky thinkers, the narrative creators, the rainmakers whom progress is dependent upon. But equally, any and every successful organisation also needs 'institution' people;

systems people, planners and landscape developers. What is then vital is that these two groups hold each other in mutual respect and learn the discipline of working in a 'joined-at-the-hip' relationship together. Left to their own devices, 'movement' people, the entrepreneurs, would explode the organisation they lead. Their ideas would simply overwhelm and bleed it dry; draining it of all resources and energy. On the other hand, the 'institution' people, the process team, would implode it, living in the kind of denial that covers over its slow decline by labelling it 'consolidation'.

A visionary leader might sometimes also be the chief executive officer (CEO) or chief of staff figure, but in my experience this is rare. I have filled the role of CEO for various wings of Oasis' work as it has grown over the years: in the initial pioneering stage of many enterprises there is no alternative. At different points, I've served in this role for our whole organisation (for the first three years of its life), for our housing, for our schools, for our international development, for our anti-human trafficking work and I'm currently doing the job for our newly emerging youth justice work. But in truth, it's never my best suit. Because of this, over the years, I have constantly chosen to give these jobs away to others as soon as I can do it safely. I am an entrepreneur. I know that what I am about to say might sound odd, but I can often see the future, which allows me to recognise opportunities and pull ideas together around them. I can collage. It's my job, my responsibility, to bring what I have to offer, even though it's often not initially understood by others, and then work alongside them as together we explore how to develop the detail of the process that will move us forward.

I have a friend who often reminds me that, as he puts it, 'We're all born into the box called conformity'. But because our welfare systems are dysfunctional – their separate cogs never turning in sync together – what we desperately need is some 'outside the box' thinking. Thinking that will enable us to do things differently and more effectively, led by those with the courage to name the box for what it is and to break out of it, rather than being bound to the tired old ways of working that keep us stuck where we are for ever.

How many projects do you know of which were initiated to revolutionise a system, but soon fell into the old trap, where the shaping and planning was given right back to the very 'the-rules-are-the-rules' people who were responsible for maintaining and policing the old one? Snip by snip, cut by cut – all in the name of reasonableness, of health and safety, established protocol, compliance and the need to not rock the boat too ferociously too quickly – the opportunity is lost in the confusion of bureaucracy. The new initiative is pushed and squeezed back into the shape of the old system.

Entrepreneurial leaders see things differently. They are heretics, and we desperately need them in every area of life, because without them we simply end up recreating different versions of the same old system – though usually with fancy new names and straplines. In the end, real transformational change only ever comes from those with such a strong belief in the core mission – the 'why' – of their organisation or community, that they are willing to make huge personal and organisational sacrifices and take risks in order to achieve it. It takes courage to challenge the perceived 'truth' of the day. This is why we need heretics like Pankhurst, Gandhi, Mandela and Thunberg to agitate and lead us. From Copernicus, who formulated a model of the universe that placed the Sun rather than Earth at its centre, to Cicely Saunders, who founded the first modern hospice and established the discipline and culture of palliative care for the dying: we have always been reliant on those who can see what others are blind to. In the words of the famous old Hebrew proverb, 'Where there is no vision, the people perish.'[30]

The legacy of any and every leader is measured by the quality of what they leave behind. It was back in 1464 that the renowned sculptor Agostino di Duccio began work on a huge piece of marble

---

30 Proverbs 29:18, KJV.

quarried from the Italian Alps. But, because of a difficult fault that ran right through it, he soon abandoned the project. Ten years later, another celebrated sculptor, Rossellino, took up where Agostino had left off. However, within months the problems posed by the massive block of marble, nicknamed 'The Giant', meant it was discarded for a second time. Still later, as an old man, the great Leonardo da Vinci was asked to consider tackling it. But having spent a couple of days assessing its condition, even he refused the impossible project. In the end, almost another quarter of a century later, it was a young enthusiast, who wasn't old enough to know any better, who took on the commission to transform the impossibly flawed piece of stone. It was a daunting task that would absorb him every day for the next two years. The townspeople laughed, well-known craftsmen mocked, they thought this young man was mad. The fact that three great sculptors had walked away from it was proof that this defective lump of marble was unworkable, but Michelangelo just kept on chipping away.

Today, 'David', portraying the famous biblical king at the moment he decided to do battle with Goliath, is without doubt the world's most iconic statue. So, what was it that gave the twenty-six-year-old Michelangelo the ability to see what others had been blind to or intimidated by? His answer, 'Every block of stone has a statue inside it and it's the task of the sculptor to discover it.'

Over the years, I've learned that for any new vision to succeed, although it will have many who are 'rationally' committed to its success, it is dependent on at least one person being 'irrationally' committed to it. That's the task of a movement leader – whether they happen to be the leader of a local grassroots community organisation or a business or, indeed, the Prime Minister!

It is worth saying at this point that this is also why the character, courage, attitude and selection of any organisation's board is vital. Their task – while they also hold its leaders to account – is to support the vision rather than to hamper or hinder it. And, besides anything else, that means experience of frontline involvement in the mission is critical to the depth of understanding they carry in their task. But this essential piece is, in my experience, often the bit that unless prioritised all too easily ends up neglected and forgotten.

A 'movement' leader's role, however, is never simply to cast the vision, but also to embody it: to be a walking, talking, living demonstration of it. Only then will it resonate with others. Only then is it capable of fuelling and renewing those who are being asked to work hard to bring it to fruition. 'Fish rots from the head down,' as they say. People follow people – for better or for worse. So, when a leader fails to 'walk the talk', inevitably a culture will begin to establish itself that is out of alignment with the vision, mission, identity and story of the organisation. It is only as an organisation's behaviours resonate with and reflect its vision – its meaning-giving story – that it can hope to develop an authentic and healthy culture.

How the leader is, is how the team will be. It's a daunting thought, but the leader matters that much. A leader's character and attention to what matters for others are crucial. So, the way they greet people or write emails, whether they bother to follow up on requests that are made of them (even when they are busy), how they talk with and listen to a junior staff member, whether they apologise when they upset someone, own up when they make a mistake, or give the credit to those who did the work rather than take it for themselves – in these small everyday actions will be the secret of the organisation's success or failure. The kind of leadership that brings this about isn't about power or control; it's never about policing the rules, the office handbook or the policy. Ethos-driven leadership is based on something very different: it's about authority rather than power and it's the only way to influence and create a culture that lines up with the mission.

A life-long mentor of mine – one of the best and most consistent leaders I have ever met – explained this difference in this simple way. He told me about his mother. Authority, he said, is derived from love, whereas power is built on control. His mother, he said, was poor, tiny and had little formal education or power, but had huge authority, which she earned by way of her countless sacrificial acts across the years. So, no matter how competent a person is, they will never enjoy sustained and lasting success unless they can effectively lead themselves, engage, influence and collaborate with others, as well as work to continuously improve and renew their skills. These principles sit at the very heart of all personal, team and organisational effectiveness. In that context, I have also learned over the years that to live with vision is, at one and the same time, to live with frustration. In fact, I've discovered that vision and frustration are the same thing. Vision is longing for what is not yet; frustration is the inevitable result of longing for what is not yet. Unfortunately, but inevitably, you can't have one without the other.

Ethos is the ancient Greek word meaning 'character'. It was originally used by Aristotle, the great philosopher, to refer to a person's character or personality, though now it's more often used to describe the characteristic spirit of a culture, a community or an organisation. Ethos is the word that describes 'the way we do things around here'. And, whether intentionally or unintentionally, every organisation has an ethos. A healthy ethos takes time to develop. But when it's invested in and is deliberately and carefully aligned to the organisation's vision, together they create the engine room for success. However, whenever ethos is neglected, there is bound to be trouble ahead both internally and externally.

The extent to which the ethos is embedded in the behaviours of those who lead and inhabit the organisation always defines its ability to deliver its work. If the culture in an organisation isn't right, don't expect to get its vision or the strategy delivered. But when the ethos is experienced and practised by everyone, the organisation gets stronger and so achieving its vision and mission becomes far easier. When people are happy at work, they tend to become people who will work hard at travelling the extra mile to deliver the vision.

When a leader embodies the ethos, gradually other team members will approach their work with an aligned attitude. But if it's not done, the organisation will become an unhappy place where staff, and especially any volunteers, don't stay for long. It is often the case that those who choose to leave an organisation are actually doing something rather different – they are choosing to leave a leader or leadership they don't believe in. The ability to successfully recruit and retain staff who are eager to work hard for the vision is the biggest 'key performance indicator' for any organisation.

It's worth saying here that I learned long ago that managing volunteers is the purest form of leadership in the world. An employee might hate their boss; they might despise their lack of people skills, their poor decision making and find the lack of clarity around the vision and mission really irritating, but they will often put up with all this because it pays their bills. On the other hand, unless a volunteer finds their work, and the way that they are managed, meaningful and fulfilling, why should they continue?

If we want the best for the children, families and communities we work with, it is essential that we do all we can for our staff first. Organisations are made up of people, which means that an organisational ethos is only as 'real' as the way it is, or isn't, lived out by the people who make up that organisation. Whenever our staff are not happy, or are distracted by their working conditions, or if there are tensions among them, we are left fighting not just the war on poverty and its impacts, but the battle to gain the full focus, attention and support of our staff.

So how do we create a different and trust-filled culture? A culture where our staff want to come to work. Where they don't take time out sick because they are too stressed, and know that they can approach their line manager about any concern and it's not too much trouble. Where they know they can trust their leaders to do the right thing when things get difficult, and feel that they can make a mistake and won't be blamed. Where they are not worrying overnight because they are scared of how their line manager might react in the morning and they can trust their line manager to have their backs. Where they are confident to say what they think, and ultimately stay because they are happy at work.

Organisational culture is never neutral, and it takes some serious intentionality to create a healthy one; one that is shaped by and aligned to the underpinning story which the organisation owns. An organisation may formally embrace an ethos, but it only works if it is real enough for every staff member or volunteer to experience it, as well as have a role in nurturing it. This requires investment: building it into every process, policy and procedure, into your staff induction, into your training and development.

The 'inside' of an organisation and the way it works always affects the 'outside' and the way its work is received. If there is a break-down – a discontinuity – or lack of alignment between who we say we are and how we behave, we will not be believed or trusted by those we serve. How we behave is the only way that others can know us. When what is going on inside an organisation is at odds with the outside image it seeks to project, it never takes long for it to be found out. In other words, how an organisation behaves with its staff, customers, clients, beneficiaries and supporters always gives away the truth about what really matters to its leaders. The apple never falls far from the tree. The goal is for an organisation's ethos to become its identity: the way that its clients, partners and service users encounter it. For example, just as the word 'Brighton' runs right through a stick of Brighton rock, so wherever you cut it or break it you can't miss it, so it should be with an organisation. Wherever and whenever you look at any practice in that organisa-tion you should experience the same behaviours and culture. It's this integrity, the consistency between who the organisation says it is and how it behaves, which is the basis on which that precious commodity trust (which we talked about in the last chapter) is built.

At Oasis we choose to pour huge energy into the never-ending process of developing new tools to explore our ethos, and we invest heavily in our staff and volunteers' understanding of it. We've discovered that we have to be both explicit and consistent about this task to make progress, and so build a focus on it, in as many creative ways as possible, into our ongoing rhythm of life; everything from our training programmes to our board meetings and our inductions to our regular staff updates. We have miles to go on all this, and always will, but we know it is important to keep working hard to get there. The Oasis vision statement is simple: 'To build healthy local communities, where everyone is included, can make a contribution, and reach their God-given potential'. It drives our passionate belief that each human being is uniquely valuable and of equal importance. Everyone has something to bring and we all need each other. Everyone matters. Everyone belongs. And because we're committed to inclusion, we're equally committed to ending inequality, injustice and exclusion wherever and however we can.

It is this vision that drives our ethos and which we sum up in our five ethos values:

- A passion to include everyone.
- A desire to treat everyone equally, respecting differences.
- A commitment to healthy and open relationships.
- A deep sense of hope that things can change and be transformed.
- A sense of perseverance to keep going for the long haul.

Our goal is that these values are felt whenever someone encounters us and that they permeate everything we do. To help us with this, we've developed what we call the 'Oasis 9 Habits', which are an invitation to a way of life characterised by being compassionate, patient, humble, joyful, honest, hopeful, considerate, forgiving and self-controlled.

Together, our five values and nine habits articulate our ethos: our way of being more fully ourselves. They form the lens through which we see all our work; a plumbline by which we check everything; a moral compass that helps all our staff and volunteers to check their motives. They are designed to keep us facing our true north. From our volunteer and staff inductions to our continuous professional development and our leadership training, to the agendas of our board meetings and the shape of our job descriptions, all we do is deliberately shaped around them. Of course, there will always be a gap between our principles and our performance; our desire and our delivery. But, in the end, what we really believe will leak out through our behaviours. And in this context, it's vital that any community organisation's ethos and values are strong enough to address the tough issues: the ones that it is difficult to talk about and all too easy to avoid; for instance, racism, homophobia and the various other forms of discrimination and inbuilt bias that we have to confront and deal with if we are to engage with and serve every child, every family and their communities in any constructive way.

So, for a moment, let's go back to those small and close-knit traditional communities that we talked about in chapter seven, and the way in which they have shaped the development of the human brain over the millennia. As inter-generationally supportive as these communities were, life in them also had other consequences in terms of the way our brains have adapted.

Our ancestors' relationship to the other tribes that surrounded them was often one of rivalry and sometimes even of outright and intense hostility. And all the evidence from those live brain scans we can now study tells us that, as a result of the way our brains have developed over hundreds of thousands of years, once again this impacts us. When we are with people whom we perceive are part of our tribe, we feel safe. But, whenever we encounter those we don't recognise as being from our community, our brain's default is to automatically raise our stress level. Remember that the brain processes everything from the bottom up – and stress levels are therefore raised before incoming information from our senses gets anyway near our 'thinking brain' – our prefrontal cortex. This is exactly why a young child will cling to its mother in a crowded room, only slowly finding the confidence to venture a little further afield, but scrambling back as fast as they can, as soon as they lose their confidence and feel threatened.

The alarming thing is that adult brains do exactly the same. This is exactly why, on a dark or lonely street, when we see people we don't know coming towards us, our state of alertness is instantly raised. It is also why the first time you encounter someone with charac-teristics that are unlike those of your 'tribe', such as a different skin colour or tone, your brain becomes alert, as it asks: are they safe or are they threatening? Are they a friend or a potential foe?

Your lower, non-thinking, brain scans the attributes of each person you encounter and compares them to your pre-loaded 'safe and familiar' categories, stored during your early childhood. This is why we all have in-built implicit biases. It's what drives racism, homophobia, Islamophobia, and multitudes of other irrational fears of those from tribes we are not familiar with. And it is why even the most sensible person can, at one and the same time, have very sincere anti-racist beliefs, but still exhibit implicit biases that result in racist comments or attitudes.

More than that, whereas planning and attending seminars on diversity and inclusion around these issues is extremely helpful in terms of the intellectual elements of learning and adoption of sensitive language, the best way, by far, to counter unhelpful old stereotypes and implicit biases is to spend time with people who are from tribes other than yours. The best way to create an organis-ation that enables this is to deliberately ensure that the challenges of inclusion and diversity are embraced within the organisational ethos, and the policies and practices that flow from it around staff recruitment, training, management, supervision and the equitable delivery of the services we offer.

On that note, although I explained in chapter eight that trust is like money in the bank and the more deposits you make, the more credit you have, leadership is also about being willing to 'spend' it, in the cause of encouraging people to move away from the old land towards the new 'promised land'. I sometimes meet leaders who are keen to tell me just how well they get on with everyone. I worry that they miss the point. The task of a leader is to lead the culture, and that will sometimes involve bringing challenge, which takes courage. But that's what all those deposits in the bank of trust are for. Rather than simply saving trust up and patting ourselves on the back because we're so popular, the point of leadership is to know how to spend the trust we have accrued wisely. Of course, as we do this, we also need to know when we're running low on capital, and when we've got ourselves slightly into the red. When that happens – and sometimes it should – you know it's time to stop spending and to start saving up again. But the point is this: it is always a leader's task to embody the ethos and to lead and shape the culture. If we don't do that, the only thing we're really doing is leading our organisations into obscurity. And, in the end, it's always our little behaviours and attitudes that give away what we actually believe and who we actually are. Behaviour always follows belief! It is those instant responses, when the pressure is on, before we have a chance to moderate our responses – the responses that come from us under pressure, just like when you squeeze a tube of toothpaste – what comes out is what is inside; there is no disguising it.

I have a friend called Dave. He's a vicar, and he tells the story of a conversation he had with a grieving woman about her mother, whose funeral he was preparing to take. He asked her if there was a story or incident that illustrated or encapsulated what her mother was like. After a brief pause, she replied, 'When I was a small child, I broke a treasured vase. It was my mum's most valued possession: a family heirloom, passed down through many genera-tions. Knowing how important it was, I screamed as it crashed to the floor and broke into a hundred pieces. But when my mother rushed into the room, she appeared relieved, not angry. Gathering me into her arms, she said, "Thank God, I thought you were hurt.'" With tears in her eyes, the woman explained to Dave that this was what her mother was like, before she added, 'My mum always told me that I was her treasure. And that was the day I discovered it was true.'[31]

---

31 Dave Tomlinson, in *How to be a Bad Christian . . . and a Better Human Being* (London: Hodder & Stoughton, 2012).

Principle ten
People become what they believe

There is an old story that Akiva ben Yosef, an acclaimed rabbi who lived in the latter part of the first century and the beginning of the second century, told about himself.[32]

Akiva had been to the village market to buy food for the evening meal, but walking home he came to the fork in the road where he had to bear right. However, lost in his thoughts he didn't even notice his turning and so absent-mindedly simply kept on going. Suddenly, he found himself interrupted by a booming voice that penetrated the descending darkness. 'Who are you? Why are you here?' Straining to see through the gloom, Akiva realised that he'd wandered all the way to the Roman garrison and that the questions were coming from a young sentry keeping guard in the turret above him. 'Who are you? Why are you here?' Akiva paused, thought, and then he answered the questions with one of his own.

'Young man,' he called up to the sentry box, 'how much do they pay you to stand guard in that turret and ask those questions?'

'Five drachmas a week,' the soldier shouted back proudly.

'I'll double that,' Akiva exclaimed. 'I'll pay you ten drachmas a week if you'll stand by the door of my house each morning and shout those same two questions at me as I rise: "Who are you? Why are you here?"'

---

32 Akiva ben Yosef (c. 50–135 CE) was a leading Jewish scholar and sage. He is referred to in Jewish tradition as 'Chief of the Sages'. He was executed by the Romans in the aftermath of the Bar Kokhba revolt against their annexation of Judah into the Roman Empire.

Who are you and why are you here? Abraham Maslow (1908–70) was a ground-breaking American psychologist, who is best known for his theory describing the stages of personal growth through which all humans pass. Maslow's hierarchy of needs, which he first wrote about in 1943, suggests that our natural needs, physiological, emotional and social, are arranged hierarchically on five levels.[33]

Listing these in the form of his now famous pyramid, he believed that these five levels of need are all biologically rooted and therefore common to every human being. He called his fifth level, which sat at the pinnacle of his triangle, 'self-actualisation'. This, he said, referred to a person's desire for self-fulfilment.

Self-Actualisation
Creativity,
personal
growth, fulfilment

Self-Esteem
Confidence, achievement,
responsibility, recognition,
respect

Belonging and Love
Friends, family, sexual intimacy

Safety
Security, stability, freedom from fear

Physiological
Air, food, water, shelter, sleep, warmth

---

33 Most psychologists before Maslow had focused on people's abnormalities and illnesses. Maslow saw things differently. He believed that people possess the inner resources for growth and healing and that the point of therapy is to help remove obstacles to them achieving this. He stressed the importance of focusing on the positive qualities in people, as opposed to treating them as a 'bag of symptoms', as he put it.

However, over the last years of his life, Maslow's thinking began to evolve to the extent that, shortly before he died, he described a sixth distinct level of needs, which he believed sat above and beyond that of self-actualisation. However, unlike all the other levels, this sixth level is unique because it transcends self-interest. Just like the five lower levels, Maslow said that this was as much part of our biological nature as the others – as much of a human need as vitamin C or calcium – and so was legitimately part of his hierarchy. More than that, he claimed, it was only through self-transcendence, as he now saw it, that true fulfilment could be found.

Maslow chose to name this new category 'self-transcendence'.[34] Self-transcendence, he said, was concerned with the quest for and discovery of spirituality through the selfless service of others and a cause beyond our own interests. Maslow described his breakthrough as 'the culmination of thirty years of work in the field of psychology'. There is little doubt that if he'd lived long enough, he'd have gone on to integrate it into an expanded hierarchy which embraced the spiritual as well as physiological, emotional and social aspects of human nature. However, in spite of this, probably because he finally wrote and spoke of his new understanding so near to the end of his life, most of the literature around his work completely misses this sixth but, in Maslow's terms, essential level of human development: the quest for the answers to Avika's two big questions, 'Who are you? Why are you here?'

It's a strange situation. On the one hand, for instance, spirituality is recognised in the United Nations Convention on the Rights of the Child as a basic human right yet, on the other, any overarching description of exactly what it consists of – especially one that would make sense at a popular level – remains hard to agree upon. So, while there's growing recognition and understanding that spiritual health is a vital ingredient of overall human wellbeing, at the same

---

34 Maslow also termed this as 'ego-transcendence' and 'intrinsic values' such as 'truth, goodness, beauty, perfection, excellence, simplicity, elegance, and so on'. See Maslow, A.H. (1971), *The Farther Reaches of Human Nature*, New York: Viking Press. Chapter 23.

time there's little consensus at either a popular or an academic level around exactly what spirituality is.[35]

For some people spirituality is synonymous with a personal commitment to a formal religion, while for others it's entirely independent of any formal religious tradition. What's more, even in this broader setting, it's remarkable how little clarity there is around a clear definition. As the 2021 census showed, the population of the UK is a super-diverse mosaic in both its religious and non-religious beliefs, commitments and cultures: a trend which is constantly increasing. This is why it's perhaps worth stopping to reflect on the original meaning of the word 'religion' for a moment. Our modern word religion is derived from the ancient Latin *ligare*, which literally means 'to bind or connect'. This is where we get our word ligament from: our name for the tissue that holds together bones and creates a flexible joint. The prefix 're' means 'again', so that together 're-ligare' (re-ligion) simply speaks of a 'reconnection' to yourself, to others, to community, to creation and to the divine or transcendent.

Just as in Maslow's writing, transcendence is the term often used in connection with the discovery of a sense of spirituality: one that creates a transformational change to self-understanding, meaning and behaviour, and brings a deeper sense of coherence to life. For many this comes in the form of a personal connection with God or some other experience of a 'higher power', whether that be through a sudden and profound awakening or epiphany, or a more 'ordinary' day-to-day growing awareness. For others this profound sense of transcendence is simply found in the act of serving others, which again creates moments of 'beyond-the-self' reflection on life's meaning.

A moment of spiritual awakening often comes to us unexpectedly; via a conversation, a film, an illness, a bereavement, a book,

---

35 The United Nations Convention on the Rights of the Child (1989) Article 27.1 states 'Parties recognise the right of every child to a standard of living adequate for the child's physical, mental, spiritual, moral and social development.'

poem or play, even a failure or a homecoming. People regularly describe these spiritual experiences as filling them with a variety of emotions: a sense of wonder, awe, belonging, clarity, connection, discomfort, love, peace, mystery, presence, self-significance. They are deeply moving and beyond explanation. However we choose to define or describe spiritual health, study after study points to the way in which it plays a critical role in the development of a person's authentic sense of meaning, purpose and joy. It provides a vital key to good mental health and wellbeing, to establishing and maintaining resilience, to dealing with crisis and trauma, and to the quality of relationships with family, friends and wider community.

But the evidence suggests that, as pivotal as these 'crisis' moments are, on their own they are never enough. Of equal importance is belonging, being known, being in community with trusted friends, and serving others. In these settings we find the opportunities to explore and test the meaning and reality of the purpose we have discovered.

For many years social scientists – psychologists, psychiatrists, anthropologists, neurologists and criminologists – have been writing and talking about a range of important human themes such as shame, guilt, repentance, justice, stigma, punishment, retribution, desire, dignity, hope, mercy, reconciliation, atonement, forgiveness, love and restoration. Here though is the extraordinary thing. All these categories are exactly the same as those used by theologians and others who write about spirituality.

It's extremely strange, therefore, that it's taken us this long to begin to recognise the depth of this crossover. Perhaps this is because most of us are justifiably scared stiff by the abuses and excesses of religious fundamentalists who've hijacked so much of this language to push their agendas of exclusion, or to focus on theories about life beyond death, rather than working to find meaning, purpose and wellbeing in the here and now. Or maybe it's because theologians speak a language that makes little practical sense to most of us, even those of us who choose a religious faith, and therefore we opt not to go anywhere near these issues for fear of revealing our lack of understanding.

Whatever its causes, the neglect of this vital public conversation around the importance of spirituality has cost society dearly. More than that, it's a price that will only continue to rise until we find the courage to explore and articulate together a spirituality around issues such as education, youth work, social care, housing, the justice system, policing, poverty and disenfranchisement.[36]

It was around the beginning of the twentieth century that psychologists first began to experiment with ways of trying to measure human intelligence. And IQ (Intelligence Quotient) – our capacity to process and apply empirical knowledge – soon became the definitive way of doing this. Indeed, for most of the century IQ was regarded as the only sort of intelligence worth having! However, as the sobering lessons of two world wars began to sink in, the focus on simply measuring knowledge as a way of evaluating human intelligence began to change. Big questions began to be asked, especially in the period following the horror of the Second World War, which began just twenty years after the conclusion of what had been proclaimed 'the war to end all wars'.

Nothing else brought more focus to this issue than the mass deportation, execution and attempted total annihilation of Jewish people in Europe: the tragedy of the Holocaust under Hitler's Third Reich. How could the most sophisticated nation in the most advanced century in history stoop to such horrific barbarism? How could Nazi Germany be, at one and the same time, so scientifically brilliant and so morally bankrupt? How could an educational system that spawned first-class students in civil engineering and medicine fail to nurture the kind of graduates with the backbone to refuse to

---

36 See the work of Andrew Millie, especially *Criminology and Public Theology: On hope, mercy and restoration* (Bristol: Bristol University Press, 2020).

use their knowledge to design the laboratories, gas chambers and ovens of Dachau and Auschwitz? However, for all this, it wasn't until 1983 that psychologist Howard Gardner first put forward the theory of multiple intelligences, and then another twelve years before, in 1995, Daniel Goleman popularised research that demonstrated that Emotional Intelligence (EQ) is equally as important as IQ.

It is EQ, Goleman explained, that enables empathy and compassion and which creates the ability for a person to be attuned and respond to the needs of others. EQ allows those who are strong in it to read other people's situations and feelings, as well as giving them an increased depth of self-awareness and understanding.

Then came another huge breakthrough. Two years later in 1997, physicist Danah Zohar coined the term Spiritual Intelligence. It's SQ, she said, that drives us to explore the big metaphysical questions: Who am I? Why am I here? Which path should I follow?[37] It's SQ that allows us to dream and to strive. It's SQ we use to develop our longing and capacity for meaning, for vision and value; to be open to those life-changing transcendent experiences. It's SQ that sits at the root of the things we believe in, and underpins the role that our beliefs and values play in the actions we take and the way we shape our lives. Zohar and others have since continued to explore SQ, asserting that there is now enough collective evidence from the various social sciences to show us that this third 'Q' is not only uniquely human, but the most fundamental intelligence. To ignore it, or to fail to cultivate it, leaves us with a lingering sense of emptiness as we struggle with an absence of meaning and purpose in our lives. For instance, in 2004, Stephen Covey, the educator, businessman and author of the world famous and bestselling *The 7 Habits of Highly Effective People*, wrote a follow-up book which he entitled *The 8th Habit*. Not only did it

---

37 Metaphysics is the branch of philosophy that studies the fundamental nature of reality and existence. *Meta* is an ancient Greek word meaning 'after' or 'beyond' or 'above'. Hence 'metaphysics' – 'beyond physics'.

endorse Zohar's work from an educational and business perspective, it also echoed the journey of Maslow some forty years earlier: 'Spiritual intelligence is the central and most fundamental of all the intelligences, because it becomes the source of guidance for the others,' he declared.[38]

Our physical, mental and spiritual health are all interconnected, and a struggle in one area inevitably leads to struggle in the others. For instance, there's a strong correlation between depression and self-worth, fulfilment and good relationships, between the rate of recovery from a serious illness and a person's sense of purpose, value and belonging. Equally, self-harming through cutting, pulling out your own hair, burning yourself, taking dangerous amounts of medication, drugs or alcohol can be the outcome of poor self-esteem and mental health issues, as can anorexia, bulimia and other eating disorders.

To spell it out plainly, any intelligent approach to our future health service must do far more to explore the link between spiritual health, physical health and mental wellbeing. We know that the old 'pull yourself up by your own bootstraps' approach to personal change rarely works. Many people in our society just don't have any boots, let alone the straps to go with them! Real empowerment comes from a sense of awareness about who you are, why you're here, and what your choices are. In the words of American psychologist William James, 'You're not what you think you are, but what you think, you are.' Here's an example.

I was more than a little intimidated as I walked into the recreation hall of one of Britain's 'Category A' prisons. I had been invited to speak to several hundred men whose freedom had been removed from them for good reason. These high-security institutions are reserved for convicts whose escape would be very dangerous for

---

38 Stephen Covey, *The 8th Habit: From Effectiveness to Greatness* (New York: Simon & Schuster, 2004), p. 53.

the public or for national security. They are filled with murderers, rapists and the perpetrators of other violent crimes.

One of the guards led me to the stage. I perched on the stool that had been provided, tried to look as relaxed as possible and began talking. However, I soon discovered that those who had gathered to listen to me were one of the most appreciative audiences I had encountered for some time. For the next thirty minutes or so I chatted about life, hope, failure, forgiveness and some of the lessons I've learnt, all too slowly, from my experience thus far. And for the following hour or so I answered questions, and listened to the reflections of members of my audience. The evening was soon over. They applauded and I prayed for them before they were escorted back to their cells. But, as this was happening, one officer slipped forward and asked me if I would speak privately with one of the prisoners for a few minutes.

Nathan was in his early twenties. As we sat there, he thanked me for meeting him, and told me about how he would have loved to have met me five years earlier, before he got himself into trouble. He then explained quietly that he was a murderer. 'That's who I am,' he insisted. 'I am a murderer. End of story – full stop. I have wasted my life.'

I asked him to tell me more. When he was younger, he had joined a gang. 'It wasn't safe to not belong. I joined up for protection.' He told me about the first time a gang member had turned up with a knife and how everyone else had been horrified. 'But the guy with the blade explained that the other gangs all carried knives and that the only way to be safe was to carry them too. We would never have to use them, but they would be a symbol of our strength, which would send a message to everyone else – don't mess with us.' Then he spoke of how one night, when he was seventeen, he was hanging around with his friends in the park, getting drunk, when a rival gang wandered in. Soon an alcohol-fuelled fight had broken out. He explained how one of the boys from the other gang pulled a knife out and came towards him. 'I recognised him. He used to be in my class at primary school. I realised he was going to stab me. I pulled my knife out and, before I knew it, somehow it was in him. I ran away. I was so scared. Later that night, I discovered he was dead before the ambulance even arrived.

'So, I am a murderer. That's it', he said. 'It's too late for me. But if I could, I'd tell all those kids who are just like I was to choose a different pathway; to learn from my story and my mistakes.' Nathan's time with me was up. He asked me to pray for him. I did. Two guards arrived ready to escort him back to his cell. He shook my hand and turned to leave the hall.

He was almost out of the door when suddenly I realised what I needed to do. I shouted across the room. 'Wait. Wait. You've passed the interview.' Confused and slightly taken aback by my apparently random outburst, Nathan and his guards stopped in their tracks and gazed back at me. 'You've passed the interview,' I repeated.

'What interview?' he asked quizzically.

'The interview,' I replied. From the puzzled expression on his face, I could see I needed to clarify. 'The job interview you just had – you passed it! Here's my name and email address, for when you get out of here. There's a job waiting for you as a community youth worker with Oasis. Congratulations: if you want it, you're a future Oasis staff member.'

We stood in silence for a moment. I watched as Nathan's body language slowly changed. His story had been subverted. His full stop had become nothing more than a comma. There was another clause to the sentence; another paragraph to the chapter; another chapter to the book – and it was called hope. Nathan had the offer of a goal, a purpose, a vision, a new meaning to his story. It was a transcendent moment.

It is time that the old suspicion of faith and spirituality gave way to a more thoughtful recognition of, and proactive engagement with, its transformative power; whether that is via the pathway of traditional religion, in all its diversity, or a spiritual encounter outside of that context all together. But its hallmark is always an immediate, and more often than not lifelong, impact on a person's entire being.

Put differently, external transformation is never enough. The impact of poverty, disadvantage and exclusion cannot be addressed in any deep and sustainable manner unless we recognise that a sense of inner hope is an essential part of the response. Our challenge is to promote a culture that not only creates the opportunities, time and space to explore this but, as part of that, embraces a new openness to the transcendent and spiritual in their various forms, as a key part of that journey.

Ece Temelkuran is a Turkish journalist and author, and also an outspoken critic of all organised religion. But, in her recent book, *Together: 10 Choices For a Better Now*, she explains that in her view finding faith matters for everyone.[39] Faith is an 'indestructible seed', a container for self-esteem, confidence and trust. 'Hope is too fragile a word for our harsh times. Faith, in contrast, is an irrefutable concept. When you believe in something, your actions are shaped by that unshakable stance.' But for Temelkuran, faith is nothing to do with gods but rather with human beings. Faith in other human beings is a tonic against the immobilising impact of cynicism. And, though she admits this 'sounds dangerous', she explains it is the considered view that she has reached by 'listening to many ordinary people around the world'.

I have a friend, Christine, who worked for many years as a brilliantly successful headteacher. Now retired, she told me that when she was a child she had little interest in education. Her background was a tough one: she'd never felt loved or wanted and was prone to

---

39 Ece Temelkuran, *Together: 10 Choices For a Better Now* (London: 4th Estate, 2021).

taking all this out on others. 'I don't know why,' she said. 'It sounds pathetic, but I couldn't help myself.'

One day, after another outburst, Christine was ordered to leave the classroom again by her teacher and to stand in the hallway until the end of the lesson. As she stood there, at the other end of the corridor she saw the new headteacher marching towards her. She was scared. The new head was a woman with a reputation for sternness.

> She stopped in front of me, and asked what I was doing there. I was petrified. I told her what had happened and why I didn't care. But when I had finished she just stood there looking at me. She said nothing. Then she cried and held my hand tight. She wiped her eyes, then walked away leaving me standing there, on my own.

> That night, I couldn't sleep. Why did that woman cry for me? No one had ever done that before. Somehow, for some reason, I must have mattered to her. And I decided that if I mattered that much, and that me being out of a lesson made her that sad, it would never happen again. From that day on I was transformed. My life changed. Somebody loved me – and it was the headteacher.

That was Christine's moment of transcendence, of life-changing spiritual revelation. And what is also clear, not just from her story, but also from many others, is that it's often the influence of another person that enables that moment for them.

It is time to begin to bring together the worlds of the social scientist, the spiritual counsellor and the theologian. Knowing what we now know about human development, to do anything less is negligent in the extreme. What have we got to say together, for instance, about the impact of hope, of mercy and of restoration in a world filled with sanctions, punishment, and retribution? What have we got to say about love, forgiveness and reconciliation in a world of individualism, broken relationships and exclusion?

However, in this vital task, just as it is foolish to ignore the often less recognised and more spontaneous expressions of spirituality, so it's a huge mistake to turn our backs on the wisdom of the traditional faiths (Judaism, Christianity, Islam, Buddhism, Hinduism and Sikhism, for example) as gateways to transcendence. Just yesterday I listened to the most remarkable story on national radio.

A young Jamaican man in his late twenties told the moving story of how his self-destructive life of drugs, nightclubs, sex, petty crime and gambling was turned around by listening to a rapper in a local nightclub whose lyrics spoke of the true values of Islam: inner peace, freedom, spirituality and a respect for women.

So profound was this transcendent encounter, he found the courage to speak to the performer as he left the stage. He was now even further gripped by the depth and authenticity of the spiritual journey that had clearly revolutionised this man's life. So, he decided to visit a local mosque. And, through the teaching and experience he had there, his life was transformed.

At first his hard drinking, gambling and womanising father rejected him, laughing at the fad of his adoption of this 'weird', 'dangerous' and 'foreign' religion. But, over the years, simply through the reality of his son's changed life and transformed behaviour, he came to the point where he too 'converted' to Islam; finding the inner strength not only to give up drugs, change his lifestyle, and get a steady job for the first time in his life, but also to begin volunteering for a charity supporting disabled children, which he does to this day.

Or take my friend Jadon. Jadon was in care in a local authority provision. Because of his persistently aggressive and destructive behaviour, he was permanently excluded from school in Year 10. His was a grammar school, but because he came from what he felt was a different background, he says he never fitted in. That's what made him so angry.

As a result of his exclusion, he was given a place at the local pupil referral unit. But after six months of irregular attendance and continued angry behaviour, he dropped out altogether. Spending his days roaming the streets, he was spotted by a gang leader, who chatted to him and offered him £10 to buy himself a kebab and chips. Jadon was hungry and so he took it. A few days later they bumped into each other again, with exactly the same outcome. Jadon says that for the first time ever, he began to feel 'looked after'.

But there was a dark side to this friendship. Too late he realised that he had been chosen, groomed and trapped. He soon found himself serving as a mule for a county-lines gang dealing cocaine and heroin. Two years later, with a drug habit himself, and cheating on his 'elders' by adulterating the drugs he was selling for them with laundry detergent to make money for himself, he was in fear of his life. But with some of the secret money he had made he managed to obtain a gun which he carried everywhere for protection.

One Sunday morning, fearing a reprisal for his deception, he sought sanctuary in a crowded church building – the safest place he could think of – with the loaded gun in his pocket. He says that he wasn't even listening to what the preacher was talking about, but that he felt what he called 'the powerful presence of the Spirit of God' and sensed his whole body 'fill with light'. He prayed, 'I'm here. I surrender.' His life was transformed. A decade later he serves full-time as a qualified youth practitioner and accredited mentor on a tough northern city estate. 'If it wasn't for that supernatural moment, I would be dead or in jail,' he tells me. 'Addiction is a spiritual problem. Spirituality is the recovery plan – it's how we are rewired from the inside out.'

It is the finding of faith, and the sense of purpose that it brings into the ordinariness of life, which very often provides that all-important moment of spiritual awakening: sometimes in a crisis of an intense, transcendent encounter, sometimes through an ongoing process, and frequently by way of the continuing combination of both.

Society is waking up again to a deep and ancient truth: there is more to being human than empirical knowledge. But in words often attributed to Albert Einstein, 'Not everything that can be counted counts, and not everything that counts can be counted.' Though we love measuring, you can't easily measure everything that matters and, if the thinking I've outlined in this chapter is right, what matters most is internal transformation. And yet, at the same time, what we as a society pursue and are comfortable to fund are services which help people exist, rather than those which will lead to transformation by empowering them to own responsibility for their lives. Indeed, many grant-making bodies will not fund what they term as 'faith' or 'religious' organisations – perhaps because of the excesses of fundamentalism mentioned above.

I recently had a conversation with a senior executive whose ethically based multinational company has provided stable and sustainable employment on a mass scale in a number of UK towns over the last few decades. She explained that it was common knowledge that although their commitment has significantly raised the level of the average household income and living conditions, as well as dramatically improved the local economies, funded schools and other social infrastructure over those same decades; the level of anti-social behaviour, drug and alcohol abuse and crime has also steadily risen. Her conclusion: 'prosperity does not create hope'. Likewise, I have a friend who has served for years now as the senior director of adult social services for a large local authority. A few months ago, he explained to me that it had suddenly dawned on him that he'd never witnessed a single case of true personal transformation as an outcome of the work of statutory agencies. 'We just don't do that kind of work,' he said. 'Our work focuses on support rather than transformation, and the thing that worries me, if I'm honest, is whether we are inadvertently spreading generational dependency rather than empowerment for anyone.'

This represents a giant weakness in all our policy making. It is time, therefore, that we had the courage to create the space for a national conversation about the relationship of spirituality to psychological and social change, because to deny its legitimacy and exclude it from public discourse is an act of self-deception.

It takes years to evaluate formally the outcomes of investment in the time, space, relationships and people to resource and facilitate the quest for spirituality. This, of course, is another of the reasons why it is so often overlooked. But at the same time, we all know that it is the people who have had the opportunity to answer those two big questions (Who are you? Why are you here?) who so often go on to become the best versions of themselves.

People become what they believe!

Afterword
We shape our systems, then they shape us!

Have you ever worn a pair of sunglasses and then forgotten that you had them on? As the sun goes down, or you find yourself in the shade, everything seems incredibly dark and gloomy, until you suddenly remember, remove them, and surprise yourself that things are not quite as dismal, depressing and discouraging as you had imagined. The lenses you'd placed in front of your eyes earlier in the day had ended up fooling you.

We all wear 'cultural sunglasses' on the inside of our head, which are even easier to forget about; but they are the lenses which colour and filter the world around us – not just what we see of it, but what they make us blind to. And, perhaps most alarmingly, for many of us these lenses end up being worn completely unconsciously, which is what can sometimes make them so dangerous.

I have a friend who worked for a huge accounting firm. One summer's day lunchtime, as we talked together in his top-floor executive office, we looked down into the street to see hundreds of staff pouring out of a building just across the road from his – another company's headquarters – for their lunch break. My friend turned to me and said, 'Do you see them? Tomorrow they'll all be given redundancy notices. It will be a catastrophe. Some will never find another job. Others will face long-term unemployment. Some will become ill – depressed, anxious. Some will become addicted to alcohol or another drug. Some will lose their relationships and families. Sadly, some may even commit suicide...'

'How do you know?' I asked.

He replied, 'Because we've bought their company, and it's being announced tomorrow.'

'But if you know that it will result in this kind of fall out, this terrible human cost, why do it?'

'Because the market demands it,' he responded.

'What do you mean?'

'Well, we are a big company, but not the biggest. We must get bigger. It is what the market wants.'

'But what does your CEO think?' I said.

'Oh, he's the one who is pushing it through, though he doesn't want it either. In fact, as a result of the takeover, he'll probably end up losing his job too.'

We shape our systems, then they shape us – and the way we see the world!

As a society we have chosen to be reactive, rather than proactive, in our political decision and policy making. We choose to throw our votes and our money at slogan-driven big ideas, and then wonder why we suffer the longer-term impact of these short-term fixes. The problem is that quick-fix, sticking plaster ideas make for poor long-term solutions, but sensible long-term policy making tends not to excite either our politicians or the public.

The problem is circular. We hold our politicians accountable for the outcomes of their huge and unattainable 'vote winning' election promises – which they make either out of their naivety or because they are smart enough to understand our naivety. But what we all know is that though they are likely to get credit for policies that get turned into legislation, in the event of eventual failure, the likelihood is that they will have moved on or moved out by then, and it will all become someone else's problem. This, of course, leads to pushing through unthought-out policies as quickly as possible, rather than getting involved in the complicated, protracted and frustrating details of how things might actually work, or not, in practice. And what's more there are countless well-meaning but ineffective non-governmental organisations, who because their very existence hangs on their undying support for the latest half-baked, politically driven idea, simply go along with it for the cash.

It is time to work together to put an end to this 'political-cycle-is-all-that-matters' thinking and the short-term, gimmicky policy making and financial wastage that goes with it. But this will require something new of government and something new of us all.

If we are going to transform the lives of children, young people and their families across the small communities that make up our big society, we have to do things differently. The future cannot look like the present. We have to reimagine and reinvent our vital community-building services: education, social care, health, housing, youth work, justice and the rest. But to do that we all have a bigger part to play. From our elected politicians – both national and local – we need a cross-party written commitment that they will lift our vital community-building services away from the vagaries of the political cycle. Instead, we require them to work together around an agreed set of core principles over a twenty-year period to reimagine and rebuild our suboptimal and failing, but hugely expensive, systems. And, to say it again, although we all know investment is needed, we also know that huge savings can and must be made through more imaginative, more joined-up, more collaborative, less bureaucratic and more transparent thinking and planning.

From the rest of us, a new level of participation is required. I grew up and have lived much of my life in Croydon. Some years ago, I remember standing at a bus stop in the town centre and reading the advert on the shelter. It was a few weeks before the local elections were due to take place. The ad read like this, 'Question: What takes just two minutes, but lasts four years?' And then at the bottom, was written 'Answer: Your vote!' What a thin, shallow misunderstanding of community and politics, not to mention democracy. In truth, we vote for the society we want to live in with our actions and our involvement, every day of our lives. Indeed, the whole thought that we can somehow absolve ourselves from community service is a relatively new one.

People sometimes ask me, 'Have you ever thought of going into politics?' By which they mean, 'Do you want to become a local councillor, an MP, or perhaps join the House of Lords?' Well, here's the thing. I am in politics. Because we are all in politics. The term 'politics' comes from the word 'polis', which simply means 'city'. Thus, politics refers to the affairs of the city: the affairs of the community. We all have an important, grassroots-level role to play in the affairs of both our local communities and our society as a whole.

Think about the story of the campaign to extend the free-school-meal scheme for England's poorest families through the summer holidays, in the middle of the Covid pandemic in June 2020. Our then Prime Minister, Boris Johnson, had been very clear that this would not happen, and despatched various ministers to TV and radio stations to defend the government's position and the reasons for it. But then came a dramatic U-turn, which he was forced into not by members of his own party, nor by the parliamentary opposition, but by Marcus Rashford, a twenty-two-year-old Manchester United footballer, and the social media campaign he launched. The Prime Minister even ended up phoning Rashford to congratulate him. In response, Rashford tweeted to his followers, 'I don't even know what to say. Just look at what we can do when we come together. THIS is England in 2020.'

We shape our systems, then they shape us – and the way we see the world!

We need a mindset change – a new set of lenses – that new social covenant to empower ordinary people and local communities across the country. It will take courage from us all, but it's time to commit to developing more mature and meaningful relationships between government, local authorities and local charities, grass-roots movements, faith groups and communities, built around trust and partnership.

Everything we know tells us that only this can transform the life chances of countless young people, families and local communities. Nothing else will work, however much money we can find to put in the budget. That is the basis for my manifesto for hope!

The Manifesto for Hope

A new social covenant

If we are going to build and fund an integrated and holistic system of care for children, young people and their families – one which is aligned and attuned to the real needs of those it seeks to serve – we have to reimagine society together.

We therefore call on central government to establish a new social covenant that:

1 **Replaces** the 'political-cycle-is-all-that-matters' short-term-policy-making approach and the financial wastage that accompanies it, with a cross-party written commitment to an agreed set of core principles, to be honoured over a twenty-year period, in order to reimagine and rebuild our expensive but suboptimal systems.
2 **Creates** a new generation of visionary 'cross-system' government leaders and officers, responsible for delivering innovative, joined-up systems with a specific focus across education, social care, healthcare and mental health, housing, policing and justice, in order to connect the policies and practices that are supposed to protect and nurture every child and young person.
3 **Builds** a deepened level of trust between government, local authorities, funders, private and voluntary agencies, and local neighbourhoods by establishing a model of collaboration and mutual accountability around our vital community-building services, designed to empower ordinary people and whole communities.

4 **Acknowledges** the central role of the voluntary sector –
local charities, grassroots movements and faith groups – in
a more imaginative, more collaborative, less bureaucratic,
more transparent and mutually accountable approach to
community development.

5 **Designs** services 'with' local people – including children and
young people – rather than 'for' them, by listening hard to
those they are seeking to serve, thus enabling individuals
and whole communities to become change makers and take
responsibility for their own lives and neighbourhoods.

6 **Realigns** funding priorities to create a new focus on longer-
term partnerships, with more core funding, and avoids the
negative competition for resources by local organisations, which
by its very nature has eroded trust, created confusion, wasted
time and resources, and fails to deliver the desired outcomes.

7 **Reimagines** the anchor role education plays in order to end the
culture of exclusion from our schools, and develops a greater
focus on the issue of childhood adversity, the nurture and
support for vulnerable children and the extension of special
educational needs support, to enable every child to succeed.

8 **Facilitates** and invests in the essential but neglected role of an
effective youth service, to work in tandem with schools, in a
relationship of mutual respect, in order to create more holistic
care for all young people.

9 **Recognises** the urgent need for education, social care, healthcare,
housing, policing and justice policy and practice to catch up
with our twenty-first century neurological and psychological
understanding of child and adolescent development.

10 **Promotes** a national conversation around the recognition that
external transformation is never enough and that the impact
of poverty, disadvantage and exclusion can only be addressed
in a deep and sustainable manner when 'the right of every
child to a standard of living adequate for the child's physical,
mental, spiritual, moral and social development', as set out in
the United Nations Convention on the Rights of the Child, is
vigorously pursued.